Jacques-Yves Cousteau

THE WORLD'S GREAT EXPLORERS

Jacques-Yves Cousteau

By Susan Sinnott

Consultant: James A. Anderson,
Assistant Curator of Fishes,
John G. Shedd Aquarium, Chicago

CHILDRENS PRESS®
CHICAGO

Founder's Medal, of England's Royal Geographical Society. Cousteau was awarded the medal in 1963.

Project Editor: Ann Heinrichs
Designer: Lindaanne Donohoe
Cover Art: Steven Gaston Dobson
Engraver: Liberty Engraving

**Library of Congress
Cataloging-in-Publication Data**

Sinnott, Susan
  Jacques-Yves Cousteau / by Susan Sinnott.
    p. cm. — (The World's great explorers)
  Includes bibliographical references and index.
  Summary: Examines the life and accomplishments of the celebrated French oceanographer.
  ISBN 0-516-03069-8
  1. Cousteau, Jacques Yves—Juvenile literature.
2.Oceanographers—France—Biography—Juvenile literature. [1. Cousteau, Jacques Yves. 2. Oceanographers.] I. Title. II. Series.

GC30.C68S56 1992   91-32960
551.46'0092—dc20   CIP
[B]   AC

Cousteau on a dive

Table of Contents

Chapter 1
Rapture of the Deep

Once before, in 1943, Jacques Cousteau and his fellow divers had been stricken by the mysterious ailment known as "rapture of the deep." It was during World War II, while Jacques, under the watchful eye of Germany's occupation forces in France, was testing his new invention, the aqualung. He and his close friend Frédéric Dumas had already logged more than five hundred dives using this underwater breathing device. They were confident the "lung" could take them ever deeper into the swirling waters of the Mediterranean Sea.

Dumas, known to all as Didi, was a risk taker, eager to push the known limits of underwater diving. He had confidence in the aqualung's ability to do its job. He also knew that, since he wouldn't be underwater long, he wouldn't have to worry about an attack of the bends. This dangerous condition occurs when a diver stays down too long, then rises too fast, causing nitrogen bubbles to form in the bloodstream. The bends could cripple even the fittest diver. What then, could possibly put him in danger?

Didi soon found out. Wearing a weight belt, he descended a knotted rope attached to one of the diving boats and entered the dark, swirling sea. As he lowered himself past the marker for 100 feet (30 meters), then 125 feet (38 meters)—deeper than any previous dive—fear quickly changed to exhilaration and then giddiness. In his mind, the boundary between land and water disappeared. Isn't the Earth really one big squishy ball? he wondered. Aren't I neither a man nor a fish but a kind of manfish? When a grouper passed in front of his mask, he barely stopped himself before taking his air pipe and offering it to the friendly fish.

Nassau grouper

Before long, Didi became so dizzy and sleepy he could scarcely grab onto the rope. When he did, he weakly took off his weight belt, tied it to the line, and then streamed to the surface. As he broke through the water's surface, the dizzying joy disappeared, and Didi felt terribly disappointed that he hadn't been able to stay under longer.

To the astonishment of the entire crew, however, when the rope was brought to the surface, Didi's belt was tied to the 210-foot (64-meter) mark. He had, in fact, smashed all previous diving records. And, more importantly than the record, Didi could now tell the world about this strange phenomenon, which the divers called in French *l'ivresse des profondeurs*, or rapture of the deep.

Divers soon realized they had much to fear from this strange intoxication. Technically, rapture of the deep is called nitrogen narcosis. It overtakes divers when too much nitrogen enters the bloodstream at great depths. Rapture of the deep, as Didi found, takes away a diver's natural sense of wariness and alertness and replaces it with a dangerous sense of power. A diver could decide he was Neptune, king of the undersea world, with nothing to fear from ordinary creatures.

In 1947, several years after Didi's record-breaking dive, Captain Cousteau and his diving team were finally ready to try even longer dives. How far down can we go, they wondered, before rapture of the deep makes it impossible to go farther?

After months of planning, the crew headed into the deep waters off France's Mediterranean coast. This time, their goal was to reach the 300-foot (90-meter) marker.

Divers at the bottom of a river

A heavy shotline was lowered from one of the boats. Along the line, at 16 ½-foot (5-meter) intervals, there were white boards. The divers carried indelible-ink markers and were to sign their names at the lowest board they could reach. They were also to describe, if possible, how they felt.

The divers were weighted down with 10 pounds (4.5 kilograms) of scrap metal, which helped them sink without wasting any energy. They were to hold tight to the shotline so they didn't sink too far, too fast. When the diver either reached his target distance or was as deep as he could stand, he was to sign the board, throw off the weights, and use the rope to guide himself gently to the surface.

As Jacques Cousteau wrote in his book *The Silent World*, he worked hard to prepare himself for this experiment. As he jumped off the diving boat, he knew

Underwater research has come a long way since Cousteau began his experiments. Here, a marine biologist carries a portable computer on board to record the results of his studies.

he was in the best possible mental and physical condition. With the hunk of metal held tightly in his left hand, his right hand around the rope, he shot down rapidly. At 200 feet (60 meters), he was struck with rapture of the deep. "I closed my hand on the rope and stopped," he wrote. "My mind was jammed with conceited thoughts and antic joy. . . . The distant purr of the Diesel [engine] invaded my mind—it swelled to a giant beat, the rhythm of the world's heart."[1]

He took the pencil and wrote on a board, "Nitrogen has a dirty taste." But his fingers felt like sausages, and the seas around him seemed so thick he could barely move. He hung for several seconds on the rope, very nearly passing out. Finally, he managed to rouse himself and descend farther. It was as though another diver—a happy, healthy one—ordered him to continue his descent. He sank slowly.

At 264 feet (80 meters), he believed he saw a glow enter the water. Had night now ended and was dawn near, he wondered. He looked down and could see the weight that marked the end of the shotline. He gathered all his strength and kept pushing down. He barely managed to scribble his name on the last board, 295 feet (90 meters) down.

The ocean floor was dark and empty. Cousteau could make out only a few shells and sea urchins. The pressure was ten times that of the surface, and Cousteau knew that any wasted energy would cost him his life. He paused a second to reflect that he now held the diving record. Then he dropped the weight and shot to the surface.

Sea urchins and sponges

Diver silhouetted against the sun

Back at the 264-foot (80-meter) mark, rapture of the deep disappeared. Jacques felt alert and in control. As he looked toward the surface with its glimmering bubbles and dancing prisms, he imagined he was on his way to heaven.

Didi went next, easily breaking his own record. He was followed by other members of the Cousteau team—Philippe Taillez, Guy Mourandiere, and Maurice Fargues. They all reached the end of the line and returned complaining they had energy to spare.

A few months later, the same group headed into deeper waters. They were confident they could easily break the 295-foot (90-meter) mark. Safety first, Captain Cousteau reminded them as they stood on the ship's deck. Lines were tied around each diver's waist and each man was assigned a diving companion, who stood on the boat, ready to act if anything went wrong.

Masked butterfly fish in the Red Sea

The first diver to plunge into the sea was Maurice Fargues, considered by all to be the crew's strongest diver. As Fargues descended, he regularly tugged at his line to let the crew know all was well. Then a moment passed and no signal. The crew looked on, horrified, as the rope slackened. As Fargues's safety man dove into the water and streamed toward the stricken diver, the crew hauled in the line. When the rescuer reached Fargues's motionless body at 150 feet (45 meters), he was horrified to see the diver's mouthpiece dangling on his chest. Rapture of the deep, it seems, had turned Maurice Fargues from a mere mortal to a manfish, who believed himself capable of breathing on land or in water.

The crew worked for hours trying to revive their friend, but they could not save Fargues's life. When the crew finally hauled in the whole line, they found Fargues had signed the board at 396 feet (120 meters)—about 100 feet (30 meters) deeper than the record-breaking dives earlier that summer.

Captain Cousteau was inconsolable. Despite his efforts to make safety a prime concern, a crew member had died. Maurice Fargues, a master diver, had given his life, and the rest of the diving world now realized that 295 feet (90 meters) was the extreme limit of compressed-air (aqualung) diving. As much as Jacques Cousteau might have wished otherwise, a species of manfish would remain—for now—a creature not of science but of science fiction.

Divers, sponges, gorgonian coral, and other sea life

Chapter 2
Boyhood and Youth

Saint-André-de-Cubzac is a market town surrounded by the famous vineyards of France's Bordeaux region. Lying just north of the poetic Dordogne River, the town's quiet beauty has long attracted visitors. For natives like newlyweds Elizabeth and Daniel Cousteau, however, Saint-André in 1906 was boring and closed-minded, and they couldn't wait to escape. As soon as they were able, the young couple fled Saint-André for the bright lights and glamour of Paris. The capital city, everyone agreed, was the place to be as the tired nineteenth century gave way to the exciting, new twentieth.

In Paris, Daniel Cousteau became the private secretary, financial adviser, and traveling companion for an American millionaire named James Hazen Hyde. Late in 1906, Elizabeth gave birth to their first child, a son they named Pierre-Antoine.

In the spring of 1910, Elizabeth returned to Saint-André so their second child could be born in their native village. Jacques-Yves came into the world on June 11, surrounded by a large, loving clan of grandparents and aunts and uncles and cousins. Then, within a few weeks of his birth, Elizabeth Cousteau packed up her handsome new baby and four-year-old Pierre and boarded a train back to Paris. It was the first of many voyages for Jacques-Yves, who once claimed his earliest memories were of being rocked to sleep on a train.

The young Cousteau family immersed themselves in Mr. Hyde's fast-paced life, following him as he dashed through Europe. Jacques and Pierre learned at an early age to adjust to unfamiliar surroundings. When they were small the two boys were brought along, but later they were often left in French boarding schools. Around 1917, Daniel Cousteau and Mr. Hyde quarreled, and Daniel went to work for another wealthy American, Eugene Higgins. Mr. Higgins was even more sophisticated and glamorous than Mr. Hyde. He was one of the richest, most handsome New Yorkers of the early twentieth century. Higgins flitted around the world, indulging in his love of horses, golf, fishing, and fast boats. All he demanded of his closest adviser, Daniel Cousteau, was that he try to keep up.

Elizabeth kept up, too, until the delicate health of young Jacques kept her close to Paris. Madame Cousteau protected her son and fretted over his health until Higgins advised the family that the best cure was exercise. And the best form of exercise, he offered, was swimming. After Jacques's first experience in the water, he agreed. "I loved touching water," he later said. "Water fascinated me—first floating ships,

The Montmartre district of Paris

Harvey's Lake in Vermont, where Jacques attended summer camp

then me floating and stones not floating. The touch of water fascinated me all the time."[2]

During one of the family's many trips to the United States, Jacques and his brother Pierre attended summer camp at Harvey's Lake in Vermont. A particularly demanding counselor forced Jacques to take part in one of the camp's cleanup exercises: daily dives to remove fallen limbs from the bottom of the lake. The dives became Jacques's favorite camp activity. Each day's work brought new challenges: "I tried to see how long I could stay underwater," he later recalled. "Then at fourteen I tried to go under and breathe through a pipe held above the surface. I found I couldn't, and wondered why."[3]

Back at school in France, Jacques was a bored and restless student. His teachers were unwilling to indulge him in what he claimed was his only interest—machines—and he responded by being unruly and even destructive. At home he built a scale model of a marine crane that was as tall as he was and designed a battery-driven car. At school he broke windows and lied to cover up his misdeeds.

When he was fifteen, Jacques bought his first home movie camera and filmed the members of his family. Some of these films still survive, including one that shows his parents walking the gangplank of Higgins's sleek yacht. Jacques loved both making and watching movies; they gave him relief from his unhappiness at school. He wrote his own melodramas and cast himself as the villain, painting on a black mustache to look every inch the part.

At school, his grades fell and everyone considered him a show-off. Daniel and Elizabeth Cousteau tried everything to get their son to work harder. They even took away his movie camera. This only increased Jacques's frustration and did nothing to make him a better student. When seventeen windows at the school were found broken, no one was amused by Jacques's explanation: he wanted the windows to look as though they'd been shot through by vengeful cowboys.

For the Cousteaus, the "shoot-out" was the last straw. They packed their sixteen-year-old son up and sent him across the country to Alsace to attend one of France's strictest boarding schools. Discipline and hard work were demanded of the students, and Jacques responded with a burst of enthusiasm for his school work. He often studied well into the night. In 1929 he graduated, with honors.

Scene in Strasbourg, in the Alsace region of France

At nineteen, Jacques's main goal in life was to travel to faraway places, and so he decided to join the French Navy. In 1930, he entered the French Naval Academy at Brest, a port in the province of Brittany. In 1932-1933 he sailed around the world on the training ship *Jeanne D'Arc*. He used his beloved movie camera to make a newsreel of the voyage. In many ways, this first full-scale expedition whetted his appetite for future seafaring adventures.

Jacques was also interested in planes and enrolled at the navy's aviation school in Hourtin, along Bordeaux's Atlantic coast. He loved flying and dreamed of a life of adventure as a navy pilot. Shortly before graduation, though, Jacques borrowed his father's small sports car to drive to a friend's wedding in the Vosges Mountains. The car was designed to go fast, and Jacques loved the feeling of controlling its speed as he looped around the narrow mountain roads. Just as he sped from one curve to another, the headlights went out. With Jacques unable to apply the brakes in time, the car flew into the darkness and crashed against a retaining wall.

The injuries were serious. Jacques was only semiconscious during those first days. When he finally came to, he learned that his left arm was broken in five places and his right arm was badly infected and would need to be amputated. The young pilot, his head dizzy with fever, wouldn't hear of it. I will beat this, he vowed. The doctor agreed, reluctantly, not to take the arm off. But he told the young man there was no possibility he could pursue a career in flying. Jacques was in despair at this news. When his parents came to visit, they found him weak, thin, and very dispirited.

Then, just as he'd summoned the will to convince the doctors not to amputate, his spirits rose to the challenge of physical therapy. The exercises were slow and painful, and many times Jacques believed he wouldn't last. Finally, eight months after he'd started, he was able to move a single finger. In another two months, he could bend two fingers and his wrist.

Just as the doctors had warned, Jacques was not able to take the pilot's exam—not that year anyway.

His arm improved through exercise, which included swimming, but to this day it remains slightly twisted. As fate would have it, though, the car accident that nearly took his life may also have saved it. Three years after the accident, in 1939, his classmates at the naval aviation school—all accomplished pilots— were sent off to war. By the fall of that year, all but one had been killed.

A German soldier in Paris while the Nazis occupied France

Chapter 3
Love and War

At first, the upheavals in world politics didn't seem to affect Jacques Cousteau much. After months of therapy, when he was able to resume active duty in the navy, he was assigned to the base at Toulon. This lovely harbor had been jealously eyed by many of France's enemies. First the Romans had wanted it. Then Napoleon Bonaparte, in a vengeful rage, had tried to destroy it. Now Adolf Hitler, too, seemed to want complete control.

In Toulon Jacques became acquainted with a fellow lieutenant named Philippe Taillez. Philippe suggested that the young officer strengthen his injured arms by swimming with him in the sea. As Jacques dove under the water's surface, he remembered an experience he'd had on a tour of duty in the South China Sea. He had watched, transfixed, as pearl divers swam far beneath the water's surface and caught fish with their bare hands. How, he'd wondered at the time, did they stay underwater so long?

Just about this time, Jacques and Philippe Taillez met someone who both attracted and bewildered them. Frédéric Dumas was a highly intelligent man who enjoyed the life of a beach bum. He never left the lovely shore of Sanary, either living on his boat or camping on the sand. The two found out that he was also an excellent spearfisherman. Soon Dumas was teaching the two navy officers how to catch fish with their hands and cook them over a fire of seaweed and driftwood. Jacques and Philippe were enchanted.

One afternoon, someone—no one seems to be able to remember who—gave Jacques a pair of aviator's goggles to try out while hunting for fish near the shore. He was twenty-six and remembers that day as perhaps the most important one in his life. Being able to see underwater was a thrill Jacques could scarcely have imagined before.

"I was astounded by what I saw," he wrote in *The Silent World*. "Rocks covered with green, brown and silver forests of algae and fishes unknown to me, swimming in crystalline water. Standing up to breathe I saw a trolley car, people, electric-light poles. I put my eyes under again and civilization vanished with one last bow. I was in a jungle never seen by those who floated on the opaque roof."[4]

Diving soon became an all-consuming passion for the three men. Jacques took great joy in making masks out of inner tubes and snorkels from garden hoses. The three felt that the possibility of deep diving, completely free of iron suits or diving cages, was close at hand. Jacques knew that, before such a miracle could take place, someone would need to invent a breathing machine that would allow a diver to sink to the ocean's bottom unhindered. The three were eager to work on

A West Pacific reef abounding in colorful sea life

their inventions, and they were certain that success couldn't be far off.

But love and war took its toll on the plans of the merry band of divers. Jacques, on a trip to Paris in 1936, met a lovely teenager named Simone Melchior. Simone came from a long line of navy admirals. The only regret of her young life was that she couldn't roam the seas like her brothers. Marrying a navy officer wasn't even a question—it was more a foregone conclusion. That her husband, too, would one day become an admiral seemed preordained.

The Melchiors looked closely into Jacques Cousteau's potential for success. Finding his naval career "promising," they gave their blessing to the young couple. Simone and Jacques were married July 12, 1937, and began their new life together in Sanary, about 7 miles (11 kilometers) from the naval base at Toulon.

Life in Sanary was, at first, idyllic. Simone fit right in with Philippe and Didi. Eventually she herself made many impressive dives into the deep waters of the Mediterranean. Her diving stopped, however, midway into her first pregnancy. Instead she watched happily from the shore as the three friends challenged each other to dive longer and deeper. Jacques was able to dive 50 to 60 feet (15 to 18 meters) in a few seconds but felt frustrated that he was unable to go farther on one lungful of air.

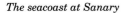

The seacoast at Sanary

Alexander the Great, in the fourth century B.C., was lowered into the ocean in a glass barrel to observe the wonders of the deep.

Jacques, Philippe, and Didi experimented with tanks they filled with air themselves. According to the best information at the time, Jacques knew that pure oxygen becomes toxic below about 33 feet (10 meters). (Today, it is a safer bet to consider that pure oxygen is toxic below 20 feet.) He also knew about the experiments of a British scientist named John Scott Haldane.

Haldane had found that, whatever the water pressure was at a given depth, the diver's air supply has to be delivered at that same pressure. The air supply's carbon dioxide—the gas that humans exhale—has to be kept as low as possible, too. Haldane had figured that, to keep safe levels of carbon dioxide, a diver needs 1.5 cubic feet of air per minute.

Early diving gear was heavy and hard to move around in. An air hose fed oxygen to the diver from an air supply on shipboard or land.

As Jacques and his friends worked on the problems of breathing underwater, they decided that the solution was to use compressed air. The next problem, then, was to devise a regulator valve for the mouthpiece. They needed a valve that would feed the compressed air into the mouthpiece in proportion to the diver's depth. It also had to keep the diver from breathing dangerously high levels of carbon dioxide.

Jacques sought the advice of his father-in-law. Since retiring from the navy, Melchior had become an executive with Air Liquide, a company that manufactured such gases as oxygen, nitrogen, and carbon dioxide. He agreed with Jacques's judgment that, since humans must breathe both in and out, one had to find

Adolf Hitler and his troops

a way of keeping the diver from inhaling the exhaled carbon dioxide. The answer, they agreed, lay in designing a valve that controlled the flow of air and water. This valve would allow the diver inhale and exhale through the same mouthpiece, without the exhaled air going back into the air tank.

In 1938, in the midst of Jacques's work on his underwater breathing device, Simone gave birth to their first child, Jean-Michel, in Toulon. The joyous family wrapped themselves in their warm love for each other and their hope for the future. But the outside world could not be kept at bay. The very month of Jean-Michel's birth, Adolf Hitler had taken over Austria and was poised to gobble Poland.

The situation in Europe deteriorated until finally, on September 3, 1939, France and Britain declared war on Hitler's Germany. The conflict, however, was soon dubbed the *drole de guerre*, "the phony war," since Hitler rolled into Poland nearly unopposed and France made scarcely a move to secure its own borders. The French, it seemed, were opposed to Hitler's aggression but reluctant to do much about it.

Jacques became a gunnery officer on the cruiser *Dupleix*, stationed in Toulon. The crew drilled often but saw no action. Hitler, after all, with his sights set on conquering Europe's midsection, had decided to leave warfare in the Mediterranean to his friend in Italy, Benito Mussolini. And, for the time being, Mussolini was staying out of combat.

Simone and baby Jean-Michel saw Jacques regularly. They had almost convinced themselves that, despite Hitler's ruthlessness, something close to a normal life might be possible. Jacques thoroughly enjoyed fatherhood and was overjoyed by the news that Simone was expecting their second child. The new baby was due in December 1940; the young family couldn't help but wonder where they would all be then.

By May 1940, the high command of the Allied forces, who opposed Hitler, was seized by panic: several divisions of Hitler's army rolled into northern France. The Germans already occupied Denmark and Norway. Britain was soon under attack as well.

On June 4, the Germans bombed the outskirts of Paris. On June 10, Italy, too, declared war on the Allies and flew several bombing raids over Toulon. Damage to the Toulon arsenal was light. When Jacques, terrified, reached Simone on the phone, he was relieved to hear that Sanary had not been hit.

On June 13 the French fleet at Toulon, including the *Dupleix*, was ordered out of the port. Italian air raids were becoming more frequent, and the docked cruisers were sitting ducks. Coded messages soon relayed the plans: the *Dupleix* was to head to Genoa, Italy, just up the coast, to open fire on the coastal batteries. Gunfire was exchanged off the Italian coast, but the *Dupleix* headed back to Toulon without serious damage to itself or its crew.

The last few citizens fleeing Dunquerque in northern France on June 4, 1940, during Hitler's bombardment of the town

Marshal Henri Philippe Pétain

The next day, June 14, members of Hitler's army marched down Paris's main boulevard, the Champs-Elysées, and took control of the city. The *Dupleix*, as it neared Toulon, received a puzzling radio message:

Keep fighting, it said, until the true French government—not the one in the hands of the enemy—tells you otherwise. Never, the message concluded, surrender your ship.

Confusion followed for the French Navy when on June 22, the French surrendered to the Germans. The British, shocked at France's swift defeat, tried to seize control of the French naval fleet so that Hitler wouldn't use it against them. The British had already withstood Hitler's relentless bombing campaign. But they had little hope of surviving a naval attack. If the Germans were able to use the large, well-equipped French ships against them, the British fleet would be demolished.

Some French crews turned themselves over to the British, but many others wished only to return to France. Britain felt it had no choice but to destroy those ships that chose to sail into French waters and Hitler's control. And so, on August 10, when Cousteau's *Dupleix* sailed again from Toulon, it was now facing enemy fire from Britain, not Germany.

Hitler claimed Paris and occupied about two-thirds of France's territory. Southern France, including the Mediterranean coast, remained under French control, with headquarters in Vichy.

France's Vichy government was organized under the leadership of Marshal Henri Philippe Pétain. To the outrage of patriotic Frenchmen, Pétain now took directions from Hitler. The fleet was disarmed and ordered to stay put.

Captain Cousteau was taken off the *Dupleix* and assigned to stand guard at a fort near Toulon. Simone, Jean-Michel, and the new baby, named Philippe, lived nearby in Sanary. Since there was little military activity in the waters off the French Mediterranean coast, Jacques was able to keep short hours and devote his full attention once again to the serene, mysterious world undersea.

Nazi troops march through Paris's Arch de Triomphe and down the main boulevard, the Champs Elysées

**Chapter 4
Aqualung**

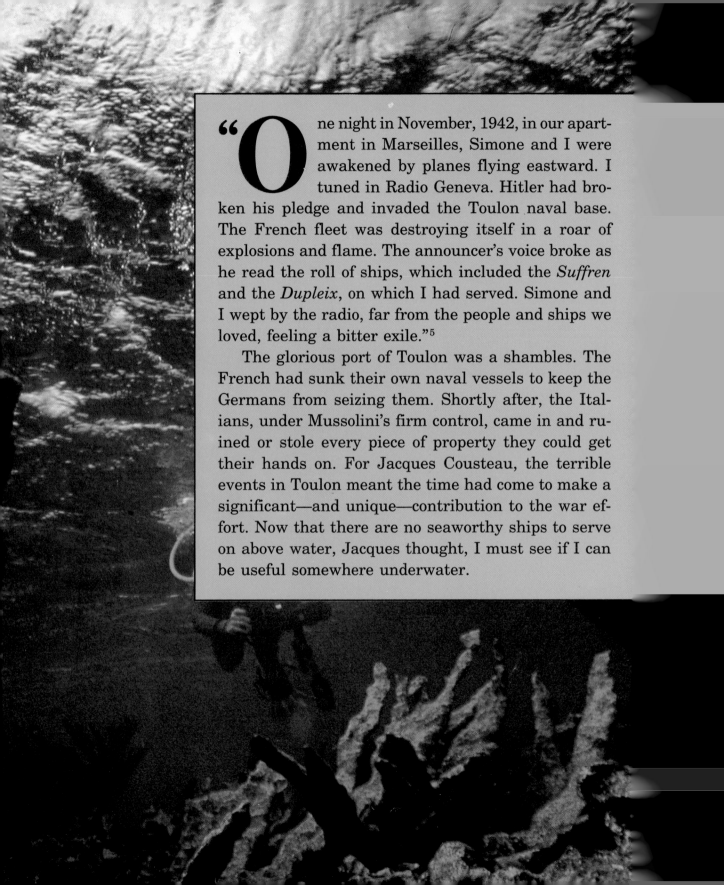

"One night in November, 1942, in our apartment in Marseilles, Simone and I were awakened by planes flying eastward. I tuned in Radio Geneva. Hitler had broken his pledge and invaded the Toulon naval base. The French fleet was destroying itself in a roar of explosions and flame. The announcer's voice broke as he read the roll of ships, which included the *Suffren* and the *Dupleix*, on which I had served. Simone and I wept by the radio, far from the people and ships we loved, feeling a bitter exile."[5]

The glorious port of Toulon was a shambles. The French had sunk their own naval vessels to keep the Germans from seizing them. Shortly after, the Italians, under Mussolini's firm control, came in and ruined or stole every piece of property they could get their hands on. For Jacques Cousteau, the terrible events in Toulon meant the time had come to make a significant—and unique—contribution to the war effort. Now that there are no seaworthy ships to serve on above water, Jacques thought, I must see if I can be useful somewhere underwater.

By this time, Jacques Cousteau had joined the fledgling French resistance movement. Led by General Charles de Gaulle, who had fled to London, the resistance worked to free France from German occupation. Both Jacques and Philippe Taillez were now expert divers. However, given the limitations of the breathing devices, they couldn't yet help with such important work as spying or laying mines. For that, a diver would need to be able to stay underwater long enough to resist detection by the enemy.

Jacques traveled to Paris and met with an official of Air Liquide. He tried to describe his dream: an air tank attached to a breathing device so that divers could swim underwater with their arms and legs moving freely. The official, an engineer named Emile Gagnan, listened carefully to Jacques and then reached for an object on a nearby shelf. "Do you mean something like this?" he asked. The object was an automatic shut-off valve that Gagnan had designed for cars so that during wartime they could conserve badly needed gasoline.

Jacques used all his powers of persuasion—and the influence of his father-in-law, an Air Liquide executive—to get funding to develop his breathing device. The problem, as Gagnan summed up, was to deliver compressed air to human lungs at a pressure equal to the pressure of the surrounding water. The key to success was to find a regulating valve that could respond to human breath. Such a valve would detect the difference between inhalation and exhalation and would let in air from the tanks as needed. When breath, as carbon dioxide, is exhaled, the valve would then close and allow the breathed-out air to escape into the water.

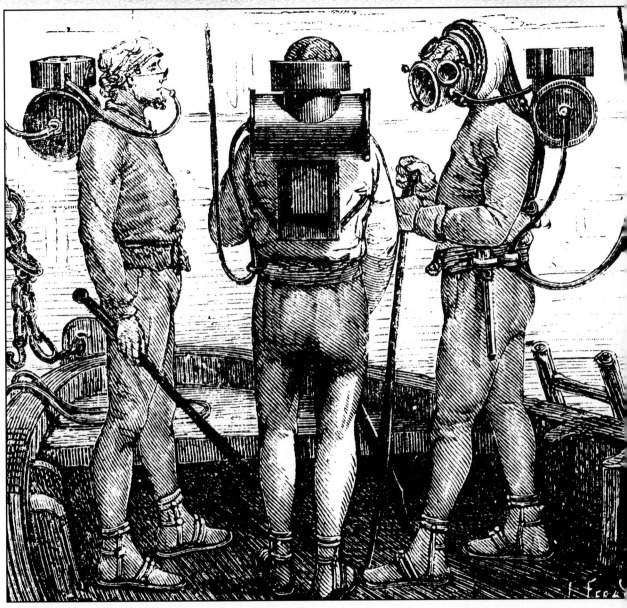

French diving gear in the early days of underwater exploration

Gagnan was so excited about the project that he set to work immediately. In just three weeks his team had built a "lung" that fit a regulator valve like the first one he had shown Jacques. In the spring of 1943, Jacques and Emile Gagnan took the new device to the nearby Marne River for a test. It was hardly a full-fledged dive. Instead Jacques waded into waist-deep water and then floated on his back.

The results were disappointing: "As long as I lay horizontally in the water," Jacques remembered, "the lung worked beautifully. When I stood up, however, air escaped with loud bubbles, wasting great quantities of my supply. And when I lay head down in the water, I had trouble getting air out of the regulator. Disconsolate, I crawled out of the water. We got back in the car and drove sadly to Paris."[6]

Soon, however, Gagnan and Cousteau discovered they were very close to a solution. They just needed to arrange the intake and exhaust tubes on the lung so they were at the same level. The earlier version had one tube about 6 inches (15 centimeters) higher than

The Seine River in Paris

Nazi prisoners racing through the streets of Toulon to avoid injury from Frenchmen lining the streets. This scene is from August 1944, after France was liberated from German control.

the other. When they were at the same level, the lung worked well enough that the two men could apply for a patent. In their application, they called their breathing device the aqualung.

Meanwhile, French resistance activity was intensifying and the situation on France's Mediterranean coast was becoming more dangerous. For their safety, Jacques sent Simone and the two boys to the French Alps. He tried to visit them often but never stayed long from his post along the coast. When not needed by the resistance forces, he tested his aqualung in the waters off Sanary.

One day, finally, all the hard work paid off. The aqualung worked perfectly, and Jacques Cousteau realized his dream of somersaulting in water—of flying in space, as he recalled in his memoirs. Still, as Jacques and Philippe Taillez dove deeper and deeper, they realized there were still serious problems. Even with a refined breathing machine, the effects of deep diving on humans were both "exhilarating and critical." Rapture of the deep was one such effect. Another discovery was that, after swimming too long in cold water, so much body heat was lost that divers became unbearably tired. The bends—the ailment experienced by the earliest underwater explorers—also struck if one surfaced too quickly after being down for a long time.

With his new freedom to move and explore underwater, Jacques was eager to begin experimenting with underwater photography. The only problem was that film was extremely hard to come by during the German occupation. Any special request for film would immediately make the Germans suspicious. Still, the wonders of undersea life beckoned, and Jacques Cousteau tried to hoard as much film as he could.

Before long, Jacques decided to try his hand at motion pictures. But getting film for movies was even more difficult than finding film for still photography. Jacques decided not to let such inconveniences stop him. He simply made the motion picture film himself. Each night he worked, without a darkroom, splicing the film together. His first short film was called *Par dix-huit mètres du fond (Eighteen Meters Down)*. Primitive though this first effort was, it did give the public their first look at the natural wonders of the undersea world.

Underwater photographer taking pictures on a coral reef

Jacques and his two friends, Philippe Taillez and Frédéric Dumas, moved quickly to another topic that had long fascinated both of them: sunken ships. Everyone knew about shipwrecks, but no one had ever seen one in its watery grave. The three divers found the ruins of an old British steamer called the *Dalton* and, with Jacques filming, played like children. They swam in and out of portholes and chased fish around the galley. Two films of these adventures followed— *Epaves* (*Danger Under the Sea*) in 1943 and *Paysages du Silence* (*Landscapes of Silence*) in 1944.

From their work with sunken ships, the three gradually became aware of the military possibilities of the aqualung. Perhaps they could organize a force of aqualung commandos who could enter enemy harbors and fasten explosives to the hulls of ships.

In November 1944, Cousteau traveled to London to show the aqualung to the Allied Navy. At this late date in the war, an Allied victory seemed to be near at hand. The Allies' invasion of France's Normandy coast on June 6, 1944—"D-Day"—had signaled the beginning of the end of Germany's power and its occupation of France. Jacques tried to convince the Allied commanders that his aqualung could be a useful tool in bringing the war to a swift end. If we had layer upon layer of frogmen mining the harbors, he argued, we could terrorize the Germans.

American troops marching down the Champs Elysées after the liberation of Paris

The British were interested in the aqualung, which they called the Self-Contained Underwater Breathing Apparatus, or SCUBA. But eventually they dismissed Jacques's plan as coming too late to be useful. Still, Jacques talked to anyone who would listen.

When France was liberated from German control in late 1944, Jacques hurried to the Alps to rejoin Simone and the boys. They then returned to Toulon, bringing with them the children of Jacques's brother, Pierre. He had been accused of collaborating with the Germans and was imprisoned.

With the end of the war came the difficult task of defusing the thousands of mines and bombs that lay undetected throughout France. Here at last was a use for the aqualung—and, the chance to become a hero not of war but of peace.

Defusing mines is still a part of naval operations. In this photo is a member of the U.S. Navy's Explosive Ordnance Disposal team helping clear a Kuwaiti port in Operation Desert Storm, July 1991.

Chapter 5
Sanary and Beyond

Jacques knew a desk job wasn't for him. The problem was to convince the French Marine Ministry of that. They had assigned him to run a processing center for returning sailors in the city of Marseilles. While he knew someone had to do such work, he also knew he was not that person. He stayed on the job a few days before impetuously heading to Paris to convince the ministry he was more useful as a diver than a bureaucrat. His powers of persuasion, and his stunning underwater films, served him well. When he returned to the south of France a few days later, he was able to tell his friend Philippe Taillez that the two now had a navy commission to perform diving experiments.

Philippe, who'd been assigned to a job as a forest ranger, was overjoyed at the news. Jacques and Philippe then offered Frédéric Dumas—"Didi"—the position of "civilian specialist." The threesome were back in the diving business. They shared a desk at the Toulon harbormaster's office and began to call themselves the Groupe de Recherches Sousmarines, or Undersea Research Group.

It was an idyllic time in the life of Jacques and his close-knit group of family and friends. The Cousteaus moved into a rented villa in Sanary, on a lovely hill overlooking the dazzling blue Mediterranean. All four of the children—Jean-Michel and Philippe, plus Jacques's brother's children, Françoise and Jean Pierre—scuba-dived for hours each day. They looked upon themselves as a family of happy beach bums.

The Undersea Research Group began working in the harbors of Toulon and Sete, removing live torpedoes from sunken German submarines. They also began the extremely difficult task of disarming mines that had been laid along the coastline, often in depths up to 30 feet (9 meters). The new diving unit quickly proved its worth to the French Marine Ministry.

The ministry granted Jacques's request to film the navy's submarine maneuvers. The result was a short documentary called *Une plongée du "Rubis"* (*A Dive of the "Rubis"*). The film amazed viewers with never-before-seen footage of a torpedo leaving its hold and gliding through the water toward its target and of a sub laying mines. Cousteau and his group of master divers constantly pushed the limits of human physical endurance. They were becoming increasingly aware of the body's chemical changes at depths lower than 150 feet (45 meters). They took great risks with their own personal safety, sometimes diving below 260 feet (79 meters). They found that the combination of the cold, the dark, and the incredible aloneness of these depths made such dives extremely dangerous.

One such risky experiment took place at the Fountain of Vaucluse near the ancient city of Avignon in southern France. The famous spring is in a crater beneath a 200-foot (60-meter) limestone cliff. As

Divers floating down into the Red Sea to examine rock formations and sea life

Cousteau explained in *The Silent World*: "A trickle flows from it the year around, until March comes; then the Fountain of Vaucluse erupts in a rage of water which swells the Sorgue to flood. It pumps furiously for five weeks, then subsides. The phenomenon has occurred every year of recorded history."[7]

No one, however, had ever figured out why this fountain erupts. Many experts had leaned over the fountain's edge and peered into the water, but nothing much had come of the countless theories offered. Finally, a retired army officer who lived near Vaucluse suggested that the Undersea Research Group dive into the spring and learn its secret. And in 1946, the navy gave the divers the go-ahead.

The crater was cold and dark, and the whole project took on a sense of doom and gloom right from the start. Jacques's wife, Simone, didn't like anything about this undertaking and begged the divers not to head into the mysterious spring. Jacques and Didi went ahead anyway, loaded down, as Jacques wrote, like donkeys, each wearing "a three-cylinder lung, rubber foot fins, heavy dagger and two large water-proof flashlights, one in hand and one on the belt."[8]

They also carried 300 feet (90 meters) of line, which was to be their only source of communication with the surface. They'd committed their signal code to memory: one tug meant for the diver at the rim of the crater to tighten the rope to clear snags. Three tugs meant to feed the diver more line. Six indicated an emergency, and the line was to be hauled up immediately.

Diver descending into a hole

Jacques was the first to dive into the spring's dark door. This was just a trial dive, and Jacques was anxious to get it over with. The dark was more frightening than he'd expected, and his flashlight was of little help. Then Jacques realized he was falling too fast and unable to control either his speed or his concentration. Suddenly, something sped by awkwardly. It was Didi, who, weighted down more heavily, was sinking even faster. Jacques could tell Didi was trying to brake his free fall and that he was in grave danger. Didi's suit was filling with water.

Jacques looked down at the line wrapped around his arm and realized he'd forgotten about the diver on the surface, who was waiting to answer calls for help. What are the signals? he asked himself. Where am I— underwater or maybe in the Paris subway station? Then Jacques's flashlight found the flat bottom of the cave. His head and ears were pounding.

He let his flashlight span around the cave until it picked out a large form floating just above the cave's bottom. It was Didi, his movements weak and awkward. Both men were suffering from rapture of the deep. Jacques's thoughts were confused; he remembers them coming all in a jumble: "I can't go back until I learn where we are. Why don't I feel a current? The pig-iron line is our only way home. What if we lose it? Where is the rope I had on my arm?"[9]

When Jacques realized he'd lost the rope, he signaled to Didi to stay put while he went up to find it. Didi thought, however, that Jacques was in trouble and fumbled to hand him some of his equipment. In the process, he accidentally sent his own guideline up to the surface. Now they had no link at all to the world above.

Jacques approached Didi and saw that his eyes were bulging and he'd nearly lost consciousness. I must find the pig iron with my guideline attached to it, he thought; I have to get Didi to safety immediately. After many anxious moments, Jacques found his line. He removed it from the pig iron and watched it fly toward the roof of the cave and out, they hoped, to the surface. Jacques clung to the bottom of the cord, waiting to be hauled up.

Precious seconds went by and still no movement from the surface. Then the rope slackened. Jacques felt sick when he realized the diver at the surface, Maurice Fargues, was giving them more line instead of hauling them in. Jacques figured Fargues must have thought they'd made a wonderful discovery and needed to go even deeper into the cave. Finally, Jacques's fuzzy brain remembered the distress signal, and he gave six hard tugs at the line. The call was answered immediately and Jacques and the almost lifeless Didi were hauled to the surface.

Maurice Fargues and a doctor worked on Didi, and in five minutes he was alert and standing by the warm fire. Jacques, who'd barely managed to climb out of the cave himself, looked around and asked where Simone was. The mayor of Vaucluse answered, "When your air bubbles stopped coming to the surface, your wife ran down the hill. She said she could not stand it." She sat alone and frightened in a cafe waiting for word of her husband's fate. Only when someone came to tell her that all was well did she rejoin the divers at the fountain.

That night, Jacques and Didi talked about why the rapture of the fountain, as they'd called it, was so deadly. They wondered if the extreme depth—200 feet (60 meters) below the water's surface—affected the quality of the air they were inhaling from their air tanks. They decided to test the air left in their tanks and discovered that it was contaminated with carbon monoxide. They had, in fact, been breathing deadly doses of carbon monoxide and were extremely lucky to be alive.

Back in the family nest at Sanary, the Cousteaus tried to keep in close touch with Jacques's brother, Pierre. The controversial journalist had been convicted of collaborating with the Germans and sentenced to execution by firing squad. The date had been set: April 6, 1947. When that day came and went without event, the Cousteaus breathed a sigh of relief. Three days later, the death penalty was lifted, and Pierre Cousteau now faced life in prison.

Later that spring, the Undersea Research Group lost a valuable crew member when Maurice Fargues drowned trying to set a new deep-water diving record. This tragedy caused Jacques to think carefully about whether he and his divers were taking too many risks. He vowed to renew his commitment to safety first. As much as he loved being on the frontier of discovery, the loss of men in his charge caused him immense pain.

One "safe" way to break the 300-foot (90-meter) mark was in the new vessel called the bathyscaphe— Greek for "deep boat"—that had been developed by a Swiss physicist named Auguste Piccard. The bathyscaphe was a kind of overblown cylinder, built to withstand pressure four hundred times that on the water's surface. The strange-looking vessel was equipped with a powerful headlight that scanned the ocean floor. This just might be the answer to exploring the great depths without too much concern for the reaction of the human body—at least that's what Jacques thought.

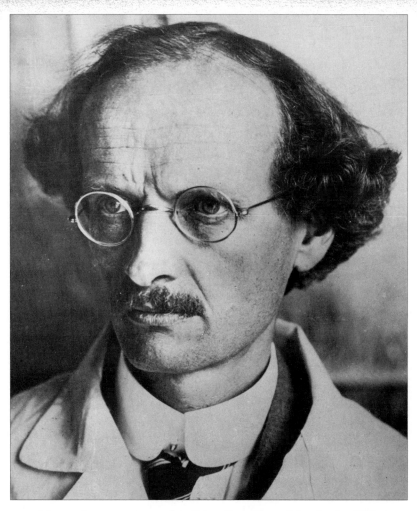

Swiss physicist Auguste Piccard

Almost everyone in his family objected. "Please don't go down in that horrible machine," Simone had pleaded. "Everyone is so worried about you." Jacques himself wasn't a bit worried and agreed to go down in what he called "a wonderful submarine dirigible."

The bathyscaphe's first deep dive took place without anyone inside. Off the coast of the Cape Verde Islands in the Atlantic Ocean, the awkward-looking vessel was lowered from its mother ship as many anxious scientists and researchers watched. As Cousteau wrote: "If the *Bathyscaphe* did not return, Piccard's wonderful idea was finished forever. A failure today meant that the dream of science of pen-

Piccard's bathyscaphe is lowered into the Atlantic Ocean off the Cape Verde Islands.

etrating the last earthly unknown would be set back decades. If the *Bathyscaphe* returned, we knew that in our lifetime, depth vehicles built on her principles would carry men into the abyss."[10]

Twenty-nine minutes after sinking below the surface, one of the main ship's crews shouted "There she is!" and 200 yards (180 meters) off the ship's bow rose the bathyscaphe. Several divers, including Jacques, swam out to inspect it. They were pleased to find that there were no leaks. But the thin plates that made up the vessel's outer shell "were rending, billowing, and sucking inward like the cheeks of an obese giant puffing on a fire."[11]

Auguste Piccard and his son Jacques in 1953 aboard the bathyscaphe Trieste *off the coast of Italy*

Unfortunately, before the bathyscaphe could be safely returned to its hangar on the mother ship, a sudden storm battered it badly, indeed beyond repair. Still, the crew was able to go inside and examine the instruments, which told the dramatic story: the bathyscaphe had reached a depth of 4,000 feet (1,200 meters). "The ironical fact," Cousteau wrote in *The Silent World*, "was that she had survived all the pressures of the deep . . . and then been knocked out of commission by a mild surface swell. We had the machine to carry men to the abyss, but we could not pass it through the molecular tissue of air and water."[12]

The bathyscaphe's design was soon modified, and Cousteau had a chance to explore the world's basement, as he called it. By this time—the late 1940s—Jacques was making great progress with his experiments in underwater television and color film. He had been able to bring back stunning shots of the world below. His success stemmed from a simple observation he made during a spearfishing outing one day.

Divers had long realized that everything is dark underwater. Even when the sun shines brightly overhead, much of its energy is changed to heat by absorption in the water. Even in the clearest waters, it is very dark 100 feet (30 meters) down.

Piccard's bathyscaphe making one of a series of dives in the Mediterranean for the U.S. Office of Naval Research in the 1950s

Gorgonian coral

The plant and animal life of tropical coral reefs is a blaze of color, but this was thought to be true only near the surface. Below that, it seemed to Cousteau, the true colors could not be seen. His crew reported that at 15 feet, red looks pink, and at 40 feet, it's nearly black. Orange seemed to disappear altogether. (Actually, orange is still visible after red disappears; deeper still, both red and orange look black.)

Once while spearfishing off the French coast about 120 feet (36 meters) down, Didi harpooned an 80-pound (36-kilogram) grouper. It wasn't a clean hit, and the animal fought hard before dying. As the creature struggled, blood poured from its wound. Jacques and Didi watched amazed as the water appeared to be stained green by the blood. As Didi carried the animal to the surface, the stain gradually changed color, until as the men hoisted their catch onto the ship, the blood looked a very normal red.

Nassau grouper

West Pacific reef environment, as it appears when lighted

Hoping to show brilliant underwater colors to their best advantage, Cousteau and Didi took a studio light, powered by a generator on their ship, 160 feet (48 meters) below the surface. When they turned the light on . . . "What an explosion!" Captain Cousteau wrote in *The Silent World*. They saw "sensational reds and oranges, as opulent as a Matisse. The living hues of the twilight zone appeared for the first time since the creation of the world. We swam around hastily, feasting our eyes. The fish themselves could never have seen this before."[13] They began filming, eager to show the rest of the world this enchanting sight.

By 1948, Jacques Cousteau's explorations of the undersea world were gaining him the respect and admiration of scientists, oceanographers, inventors, and photographers around the world. His early film, *Eighteen Meters Down*, had won him a special award at the Cannes Film Festival. Now he was eager to make an underwater film in color. People would scarcely believe their eyes, the eager filmmaker told potential investors.

Jacques looked excitedly toward the future—he knew there was so much to study and explore and so many uses for the aqualung. He and his crew made hundreds of deep dives, and each one brought up as many new questions as answers.

Photographing a school of goatfish in the Caribbean

Chapter 6
Calypso

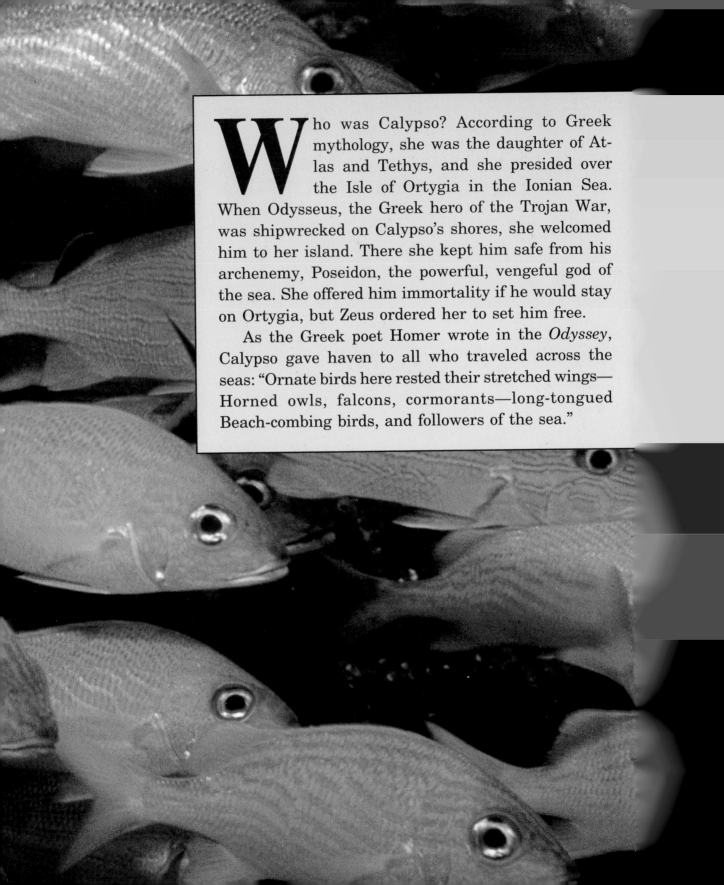

Who was Calypso? According to Greek mythology, she was the daughter of Atlas and Tethys, and she presided over the Isle of Ortygia in the Ionian Sea. When Odysseus, the Greek hero of the Trojan War, was shipwrecked on Calypso's shores, she welcomed him to her island. There she kept him safe from his archenemy, Poseidon, the powerful, vengeful god of the sea. She offered him immortality if he would stay on Ortygia, but Zeus ordered her to set him free.

As the Greek poet Homer wrote in the *Odyssey*, Calypso gave haven to all who traveled across the seas: "Ornate birds here rested their stretched wings— Horned owls, falcons, cormorants—long-tongued Beach-combing birds, and followers of the sea."

Cousteau aboard his new research ship Calypso *bound for its maiden voyage in the Red Sea*

Perhaps Jacques Cousteau included himself among the followers of the sea when he chose the name *Calypso* for his research ship. He had dreamed and talked about a vessel built for divers and oceanographic research since 1944 but had often been laughed at. "Become an admiral!" said one navy official. "Then you might get your ship!"[14] But Jacques didn't care about advancement. He wanted to roam the seas on his own ship, not the navy's.

After the war, Jacques intensified his search for the right vessel. He asked a wealthy friend to help finance the project and the friend, in turn, asked one of his colleagues. Jacques believed that refitting a

The grand harbor at Valletta, Malta

navy ship would be the best way to go. He began searching for a minesweeper. This type of ship was built to withstand difficult conditions, and, in the late 1940s, they were in surplus in many naval ports.

Jacques was told that Malta was the place to look for his ship, so off he went to this island south of Sicily. There he spotted his dear *Calypso*. When he saw it in Valletta harbor, he wrote, "the search was over." Everything about *Calypso* seemed just right—not too big, yet sturdy, with two engines, and able to reach a speed of 10.5 knots (11.5 miles per hour). Even the price was right. With a grant from a wealthy Englishman, it was quite affordable.

Now the only stumbling block to Jacques's dream of leading a research vessel through the world's seas was the French Navy. Captain Cousteau was still in it, and he would have to take a leave of absence if he was going to sail his *Calypso* around the world. The navy was reluctant to give its blessing to such an independent venture. "Look here, young man," an admiral told him sternly. "The Navy cannot detach people for service to themselves."[15] But in the end, that's exactly what Jacques convinced the navy to do.

Calypso was taken to the Mediterranean port of Antibes for a complete refitting. Jacques oversaw the work, making sure that his ship provided comfortable quarters for the crew. He also made sure it was equipped with many of the features he'd dreamed about. That included a diving platform and an underwater observation chamber on the front of the ship.

The process of refitting the *Calypso* took almost everything the Cousteau family had. Simone Cousteau sold valuable antique jewelry, while her father asked friends and business associates for outright gifts. The situation was helped when Jacques formed a nonprofit corporation, Compagnies Océanographique Françaises (COF), to oversee the grants, donations, and money earned from his magazine articles, books, and films.

On November 24, 1951, *Calypso*'s first full-blown expedition left Toulon for the Red Sea, the waters between East Africa and the Arabian Peninsula. Because the COF didn't have the money for a full crew, friends and family members pitched in once again. Quarters were cramped, but the atmosphere was warm and happy. From the first, Captain Cousteau made it clear that the crew of the *Calypso* must work as a team.

Twobar anemonefish, domino damselfish, and carpet anemone in the Red Sea

As the team's coach, Cousteau stressed safety above all else. He did not hesitate to delay projects in order to test and retest equipment. The first law of the *Calypso* and its captain was: Never take unnecessary risks.

On December 5, the *Calypso* sailed through the Suez Canal, connecting the Mediterranean and the Red Sea. Nearly two weeks later, they reached the Farasan Islands near the coasts of Saudi Arabia and Yemen, which are known for their spectacular coral reefs. The group set up a base camp and several crew members camped on an uplifted part of a reef. Meanwhile, the ship traveled the area performing experiments.

Queen triggerfish

Captain Cousteau himself was among the first to dive into the deep waters off the Farasan Islands. The divers met up with so many unknown species of plant and animal life that the biologists on board had trouble thinking up so many new names. Among the new names they chose for plant species were *cousteaui* and *calypseus*.

One day like many others, Jacques and his divers drifted effortlessly over clumps of sea lavender and orange coral and past electric blue triggerfish, silver sardines, and purple and black coral fish. The reef ended suddenly with a ledge overhanging a blue abyss. As Didi peered into a small opening in the cliff, Jacques noticed a shark swimming toward his friend. Jacques

Sand shark

tried to call out a warning through his mouthpiece, but Didi didn't hear. Then just as suddenly, the huge animal turned and swam away. As Captain Cousteau noted later in an article for *National Geographic*, the shark seemed only mildly curious about this strange-looking manfish. The captain guessed that humans have more to fear from sharks scavenging near the water's surface than from those 100 feet (30 meters) below.

The expedition was a benefit to both scientists and underwater photographers. The scientists were able to collect and catalogue new life forms. And the photographers, including Cousteau himself, experimented with underwater lighting and ways of lowering cameras to the ocean floor.

As Captain Cousteau well understood, the photographs they would bring back were crucial in persuading the French government and international foundations to fund future *Calypso* endeavors. And he knew that if he were ever to realize his dreams of traveling the world's seas and filming to his heart's content, he would need money—lots of it, and in a steady supply. So when he headed to the United States in 1952, it was both to spread the word of the *Calypso*'s work and to raise money for its future missions.

In Washington, Jacques met with Gilbert Grosvenor, the president, editor, and son of the founder of the National Geographic Society. In 1952 the society had an international membership of three million people, all of whom received the well-known monthly magazine. Mr. Grosvenor looked at the pictures Jacques had brought back from the Red Sea and agreed to publish an article on undersea exploration.

When Mr. Grosvenor asked about the future plans of the *Calypso* and crew, Jacques was ready with his answer. He wanted to a take a three- or four-year trip to assess the world's ocean, literally from the bottom up. We know almost nothing, the captain insisted, about life beyond 600 feet (180 meters). And as for marine life, our knowledge is at the most preliminary stage.

Gilbert Grosvenor couldn't give the persuasive Frenchman an answer, but he was clearly impressed by his eloquence. Jacques then traveled to New York, where he talked to filmmakers and TV broadcasters. He and his American assistants tried to convince the CBS network to make three 90-minute films. Clearly there was tremendous interest in the discoveries made by the captain and crew of the *Calypso*.

Gilbert M. Grosvenor, president and chairman of the National Geographic Society

Cousteau in 1953

But keeping the *Calypso* afloat took more than promises for the future. It took energy, persuasiveness, and a willingness to do anything to find funds. Someone suggested that, if Cousteau needed money, he should take his ship and divers on a hunt for sunken treasure. Jacques did not laugh off the suggestion. He considered it carefully and agreed that treasure-hunting might be just the thing.

Cousteau and crew members showing two bronze statuettes of the second century B.C., found during an expedition off the Greek islands of the Aegean Sea

The Grand Congloue is a huge rock that rises from the Mediterranean just south of the harbor of Marseilles, France. A Roman freighter had sunk near the Grand Congloue around 230 B.C., and Cousteau and his crew discovered the ship's remains off the southern face of the rock. During much of the summer of 1952, the *Calypso* sat near the Grand Congloue, serving as a diving board for its crew of treasure hunters. The haul was impressive: thousands of wine amphoras (jars) and two-handled storage jugs, tiles, and coins.

That fall, good fortune came in other forms. Jacques received word from National Geographic that they would indeed fund his next mission. Then, with such a prestigious organization pledging its support, oth-

Diver exploring a shipwreck

ers—the French Navy and the Academy of Science, for example—fell in line, too.

In the early months of 1953, Jacques was back in the United States visiting with his many contacts in government, academics, and the media. In New York City, he met with James Dugan. Out of their talks came *The Silent World*, a book based on logs kept by both Jacques and Didi during the past fifteen years. The book, which begins with the early war years and takes the reader through to the *Calypso*'s Red Sea expedition, attempts to describe the undersea world from the diver's point of view. The book struck a responsive chord among American readers, who were just beginning to think of the ocean as something more than a resource to be exploited.

The Silent World brought Jacques Cousteau international attention. One day, an executive of the British Petroleum Corporation paid a visit to the *Calypso*, which was temporarily docked in Marseilles. He'd read *The Silent World* and had been thinking long and hard about the possibility of using men diving in aqualungs to help look for new oil reserves. Jacques, eager for the *Calypso* to earn her keep, quickly agreed to British Petroleum's terms. He then doubled the size of his crew and headed for the waters of the Persian Gulf.

One of the men accompanying Cousteau on this latest trip was a twenty-year-old filmmaker named Louis Malle. Jacques spoke often of his desire to "film it all," and so he eagerly took on the filmmaker. Malle was not only talented and eager but was also an excellent scuba diver.

French filmmaker Louis Malle

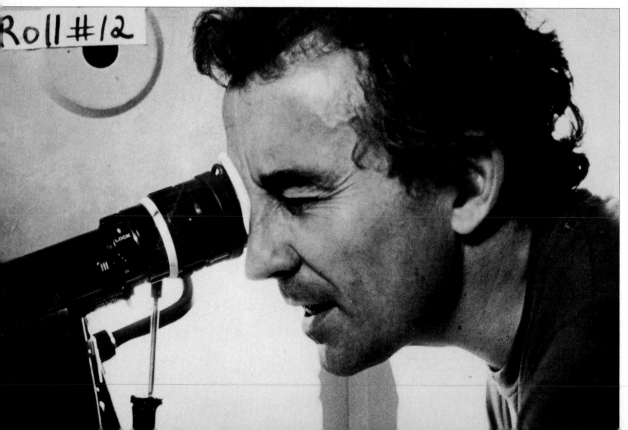

And so, on January 7, 1954, the crew of the *Calypso* left on their second major expedition. After leaving the coral reefs of the Red Sea, they sailed around the coast of Yemen, into the Gulf of Oman and toward Abu Dhabi, which was under the control of the British Petroleum Corporation. For two months the crew engaged in their most back-breaking assignment yet: chiseling rock samples from ledges 150 feet (45 meters) under water. The temperature on land was brutally hot, yet the waters were cold and filled with sharks and venomous sea snakes. The divers collected a total of 150 rock samples and sent them off to labs for analysis. After the samples were analyzed, officials of British Petroleum were able to tell where to drill for offshore oil.

Diver in a "shark cage"

When the crew's work in Abu Dhabi was finished, the *Calypso* headed toward the Indian Ocean and the eastern coast of Africa. For the next several months, the *Calypso*'s crew studied and filmed whales and sharks. They tested many new techniques that helped assure underwater photography's safety. The camera might capture a diver drifting effortlessly from cave to cave, but the effort required for filming such a scene was enormous. Artificial light was essential, and that meant lamps and cables and divers to carry them.

In the shark-infested waters of the Indian Ocean, protective cages were a necessity. The stress of this six-month-long expedition left the divers tired and drained. When Captain Cousteau finally ordered the *Calypso* back into the Mediterranean and home to France, he indulged his weary crew's need for several days of no work and all play. A card game began somewhere in the Gulf of Suez and didn't stop until the *Calypso* reached its home port of Toulon.

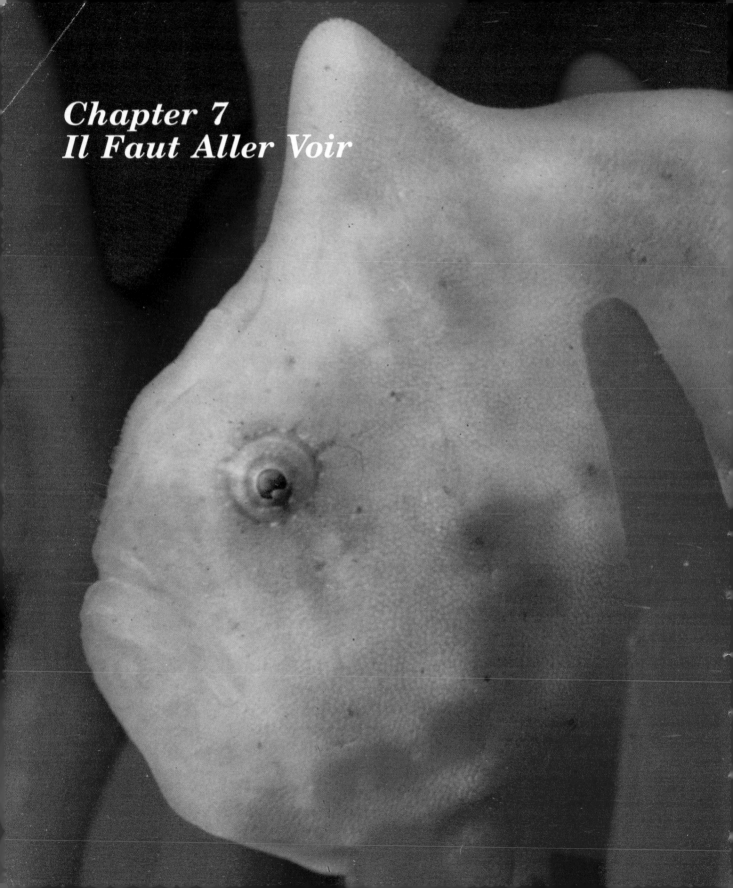

"You like the sea, Captain?"

"The sea is all. Its breath is pure and healthy. . . . Beneath the sea, that's the only place for independence! There I acknowledge no master! There I am free!"

—Captain Nemo in Jules Verne's 20,000 Leagues under the Sea

Even in the early days, when money was scarce and pay was low, Captain Cousteau had no trouble recruiting new divers for *Calypso*'s expeditions. He could promise them nothing more than hard work, sunburn, insect bites, moments of extreme loneliness— and, of course, adventure. But young men lined up for the chance to serve on *Calypso*. In the 1940s and 1950s, there were many young Frenchmen who felt the world war had denied them the chance to be wild and daring. They were eager to explore the unknown. "I cannot help thinking," Captain Cousteau once wrote, "that the men of the *Calypso* resemble, in many ways, those of Jules Verne's [submarine] *Nautilus*—men who had been wounded by life on land, and who thereafter put their trust in the sea."[16]

Indeed, as schoolboys, all the divers had read Jules Verne's classic story of the mad Captain Nemo and his strange underwater vessel *Nautilus*. And they all re-read the passages in Cousteau's own copy as *Calypso* took them into the deep waters of the world's oceans.

Captain Cousteau always looked for two qualities in his recruits: competence and companionship. "Competence" meant being willing and able to become the best possible diver. The work of a *Calypso* crew member could be extremely dangerous, and everyone had to be able to think and perform quickly. "Companion-

A giant octopus attacking the Nautilus *in Jules Verne's* Twenty Thousand Leagues Under the Sea

ship" was harder to define but no less important. Diving, Cousteau would stress, is not for the loner. You need to be aware of others and to rely on them. Likewise, the long weeks and months on board ship required a crew member who felt a part of the team both at work and at play. "You have to be a good diver and something else," Cousteau once wrote. "People who come are either rejected or accepted by the rest of the crew. We lose about one person a year, but people who are accepted and cherished by their friends will stay, maybe, twenty or twenty-five years. It's like a transplant, an organ transplant. It is rejected or accepted. That's the way we make our team."[17]

Captain Cousteau demanded loyalty—how else could the team work?—and in return he made his crew's safety his main concern. He spent precious resources on every safety device invented. And he was sure to tell anxious investors and sponsors that safety-related delays were to be expected. He would never consider the life of one of his crew less important than valuable cargo or a film production deadline. The death of Maurice Fargues in 1947 and the drowning of another expert diver, Jean-Pierre Serventi, in 1952 were tragic events that Captain Cousteau took to heart and insisted everyone learn from.

And, Calypso's crew knew there was no one more dedicated or hard-working than Captain Cousteau. The phrase they remember coming from his lips most often was "Il Faut Aller Voir"—"We must go see for ourselves." It was Cousteau's way of saying, "Let's push ourselves farther, let's not give up here, there must be something more we can explore." The captain's natural curiosity spread to the entire crew and encouraged everyone to learn more about the undersea world.

By the end of 1953, *The Silent World* had sold nearly one-half million copies, and Cousteau was becoming well-known by millions. Increasingly, international fame tried to force open the tight-knit atmosphere on board ship. Fame could easily have changed the spirit of dedication on board. But Captain Cousteau's compassionate leadership and his crew's commitment kept *Calypso* on track. Everyone was affected by the attention. Yet their devotion to duty helped them keep their minds on *Calypso*'s mission—the exploration of the world's seas.

The captain decided to use the money earned from his book sales to produce a full-length documentary film, also to be called *The Silent World*. Cousteau knew that the footage, shot with the young filmmaker Louis Malle, was good. But their technique and equipment was always improving, and he knew they could get even more stunning shots on *Calypso*'s next voyage.

Calypso was in drydock for several months during 1954-1955, receiving a badly needed overhaul. All equipment and data were checked and rechecked, and the crew's quarters were made more comfortable. In an effort to get the undersea photographs they wanted, Didi and Louis Malle purchased new lighting equipment, a new type of film, and buoys of all kinds. They spend months adapting cameras to undersea use.

"We had to make the underwater cameras ourselves because there was nothing we could use at the time," he reported.[18]

They also hired several more photographers and cinematographers. By the time *Calypso* was ready to sail on its next expedition in March 1955, the research ship was the best-equipped movie studio on the high seas.

Goggle-eye (a fish) in the Red Sea

In March 1955, the almost-new *Calypso* left Toulon for a 13,700-mile (22,000-kilometer) voyage. This venture took the crew through the Red Sea to the Indian Ocean, south to the Seychelles Islands, and finally to tiny Assumption Island. The trip went smoothly except that, between Madagascar and the Seychelles island of Aldabra, *Calypso* was battered by the trade winds. Both captain and crew struggled to keep *Calypso* on course. Finally Cousteau decided to anchor in a natural harbor, protected from the lashing winds, off the west coast of Assumption Island.

As *Calypso* glided into the calm waters, the men noticed the water was crystal clear. One diver, Jean Delmas, began filling the air tanks before the ship had even dropped anchor. As Cousteau describes in *The Living Sea*, "Delmas treated himself to the first dive. He went head down through the looking glass into the most enormous vistas he had ever scanned in the underwater world. The sea was transparent for two hundred feet in any direction. Delmas had been with the *Calypso* in the Red Sea reefs . . . but had not seen anything approaching the scenes that Assumption Reef offered to the human eye. The corals were richer. The fish were thicker and had no fear."[19]

Delmas urged Captain Cousteau not to move *Calypso* on to the larger island of Aldabra before all the divers could inspect the astonishing waters. "This is the place to make friends with fish," Delmas proclaimed, and the crew stood in line for their turns to plunge into the waters. The divers were urged not to do anything that might affect the fishes' friendliness toward their human guests. "No fishing except by the cook" became the rule.

Two by two the divers sampled the "waters from paradise," as they called them. Luis Marden, a photographer for *National Geographic*, could barely speak when he emerged. "Jacques," he sputtered, "it is incredible down there. It is the ocean turned inside out. When I tried to take close-ups of the fish, they came too near to stay in focus. When I backed off, they came with me."[20]

Jacques decided finally that he had to see these waters for himself and dove in. He was, he wrote, immediately enslaved by the beauty of the underwater scene. There, just off the reef's bank, were all the species of fish they'd encountered before, plus many kinds they'd never before seen.

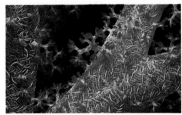

Soft coral

The *Calypso* didn't leave that day, or the next, as planned. Instead it stayed forty days, rationing fresh water and food in order to stretch out the visit. The ship was anchored there so long, in fact, that fish began to think of it as an island, which they clung to for shelter. The divers became so attached to the fish that they were eager to plunge into the waters each day to greet them. One fish, a 60-pound (27-kilogram) grouper, became so friendly that he waited every morning at the divers' ladder. Then he followed the men, nudging them and nibbling their fins. At the end of deep dives, when divers must decompress at 30 feet (9 meters) to avoid an attack of the bends, the grouper, which the men named Ulysses, would playfully swim in and out among legs and arms. When a diver climbed onto the ship, Ulysses would wait just under the surface, looking like a kid watching his best friend going home for dinner after a long day of play.

The crew of *Calypso* had seen groupers before, of course, even in the Mediterranean. But closer to civilization, these fish had become wary of humans and would stay far away. Ulysses, on the other hand, seemed to feel there was little risk in playing with these strange-looking menfish. It even seemed to the divers that Ulysses thought he could call the shots. In a friendly mood, he would let the divers scratch his head. But when he felt wronged by the humans, he would show his temper—or so it seemed, at least. He often swam into the middle of Louis Malle's or Luis Marden's camera shots and they would have to push him away. Then he would leave, flapping his tail powerfully as if in disgust.

When Captain Cousteau decided that *Calypso* must visit the nearby island of Aldabra, the ship left its mooring for four days. All the divers hated to go, even for a short while, but they waved good-bye to Ulysses, promising him they'd return in a few days.

The next afternoon, as the boat passed out of the bay, they were greeted by a fishing boat that belonged to one of the few inhabitants of Assumption Island. The fisherman gave a friendly greeting and held up a huge fish that he was clearly pleased to have just caught. Sure that they recognized Ulysses, the divers were inconsolable for the rest of the day. If we had not been so friendly with Ulysses and brought meat to him, they lamented, he would have had no interest at all in a hook baited with food from humans. They had, they felt, caused the extraordinary fish's death.

When *Calypso* returned to Assumption in a few days, the crew dreaded the first dive, sure that their friend Ulysses would be nowhere in sight. As the ship maneuvered into its anchoring spot, one of the divers impatiently plunged into the water wearing only a mask and fins. He dove toward the reef and sprang back out of the water, yelling "Ulysses is here!" Then, when another crew member lowered the diving ladder, the huge fish swam right to the bottom waiting for his friends to come into the water to play.

When *Calypso* finally left, there was some talk of trying to bring Ulysses back to France. The bosun— the crewman in charge of ship maintenance—proposed building a pool lined with a tarpaulin on deck for Ulysses. Captain Cousteau admitted that he was tempted. But finally, reason won out. Life for Ulysses in France could never be so joyous as in the untouched waters off Assumption Island.

Louis Malle in 1988. Malle became an outstanding director of French "new wave" cinema.

Back in France, Cousteau, Louis Malle, and two film editors began sorting through the hours of film shot on *Calypso*'s expeditions. They worked for months looking for the perfect mix of shots for their hour-and-a-half film. The two men disagreed somewhat on the approach the film should take: Jacques wanted a true documentary, showing both the underwater images and the work of *Calypso*'s crew. Louis Malle, on the other hand, wished for a combination of art and poetry. In the final version, the film's opening shot of air bubbles disturbing the quiet blue water is Malle's idea. The next image, of the strange-looking menfish climbing the ladder to *Calypso*'s deck, is Cousteau's.

Le Monde du Silence (*The Silent World*), co-directed by Jacques Cousteau and Louis Malle, had its world premiere at the 1956 Cannes Film Festival. Its first audience was stunned by the film's technical mastery, the undersea life forms, and the dazzling colors. The film was pronounced a work of rare beauty and won the festival's highest award. A year later in Hollywood, *The Silent World* also won an Oscar for best documentary. For both directors, these honors marked just the beginning of long, successful filmmaking careers. (Louis Malle went on to direct several classic French films, including *Murmur of the Heart* and *Lacombe, Lucien*. He later directed several American hits as well, including *Pretty Baby* and *Atlantic City*.)

Cousteau, his wife Simone, and their pet dachshund aboard the Calypso *in New York Harbor in 1959 during the International Oceanographic Congress*

Now that Captain Jacques-Yves Cousteau had become an internationally successful author and film-maker, the French Navy wasn't sure what to do with him. Despite his well-known adventures at sea, he was, at the age of forty-seven, the lowest ranked officer among all his classmates from the Naval Academy. Now that his name was practically a household word, his superiors felt embarrassed by the situation.

Fortunately, Jacques saved the navy from having to decide what to do next. In 1957, he resigned his post. The decision was difficult: he had been a navy man for twenty-seven years and had enjoyed the security of his salaried position. But the navy is a tradition-bound branch of service, and Jacques liked to live on the frontier. After a few years of life on board *Calypso*, he and Simone agreed they had little use for the navy's stuffy ways. Now they both really only felt at home on board the *Calypso*.

Happily, a new opportunity presented itself almost immediately. Prince Rainier, the handsome ruler of tiny Monaco, was searching for a new head of Monaco's respected Oceanographic Institute. Why should he consider anyone other than the famous undersea explorer, who lived less than a hundred miles (160 kilometers) down the road in Sanary? Cousteau accepted the offer at once and plunged into his new assignment with his typical energy and zeal.

In the summer of 1959, Captain Cousteau sailed *Calypso* to New York City, where the ship was greeted with sirens and waterworks. The ship and crew were in New York to take part in the first International Oceanographic Congress. Thousands of scientists, officials, and journalists visited the research ship, treating its captain and crew as stars.

The Oceanographic Institute in Monaco, high on a cliff over the Mediterranean Sea

The name and face of Jacques-Yves Cousteau were, in fact, everywhere—even on the cover of *Time* magazine. Everyone, it seemed, knew about this tall, skinny Frenchman. And, as *Time* reported, one million Americans had taken up scuba diving. Captain Cousteau was eager to turn his popularity to good use: that is, to use the profits from his many films, books, and lectures to increase popular and financial support for his undersea projects.

By 1960, scientists and oceanographers were just discovering the word "pollution." When Captain Cousteau gathered up the full force of his fame and power and decided to protest the French army's dumping of nuclear wastes in the Mediterranean, many were stunned. Weren't the world's oceans just gigantic dumping grounds for humans' various waste products? Cousteau boldly said no, and he took whatever opportunity he could to say so. The World Underwater Federation was an organization of divers from Europe and North America that elected Cousteau as its head. As president, he proposed to the federation that the disposal of nuclear wastes in the sea be stopped.

As the decade of the 1960s began, Captain Cousteau's fame was at its peak, and he used his position to put the world on alert. Another cause for concern was atomic testing, which was being conducted in remote ocean areas around the world. Oceanographers worried about the effects of dusting the world's seas with radioactive fallout. But with relations between the United States and the Soviet Union at the freezing point, would anyone hear Jacques Cousteau's voice over the clamor for more weapons and atomic tests? As the space race also quickened, oceanographers couldn't help but wonder whether the hunger for knowledge about the world's oceans would disappear.

In a White House Rose Garden ceremony, in April 1961, President John F. Kennedy presented Jacques-Yves Cousteau with the National Geographic Society's gold medal. The president spoke of how the great explorer had "opened up the ocean floor to man and to science." The crowd of family, friends, and French government officials beamed with pride at the many accomplishments of this distinguished man.

Cousteau examined the gold medal, probably reflecting on its poetic message: "To earthbound man he gave the key to the silent world." The undersea world, he may have been thinking, may be silent, but beware, its chief spokesman has a booming voice and a watchful eye.

Cousteau admires the National Geographic Society gold medal with President John F. Kennedy in the White House Rose Garden. Next to him is the society president at the time, Melville Bell Grosvenor.

Chapter 8
The Price of Fame

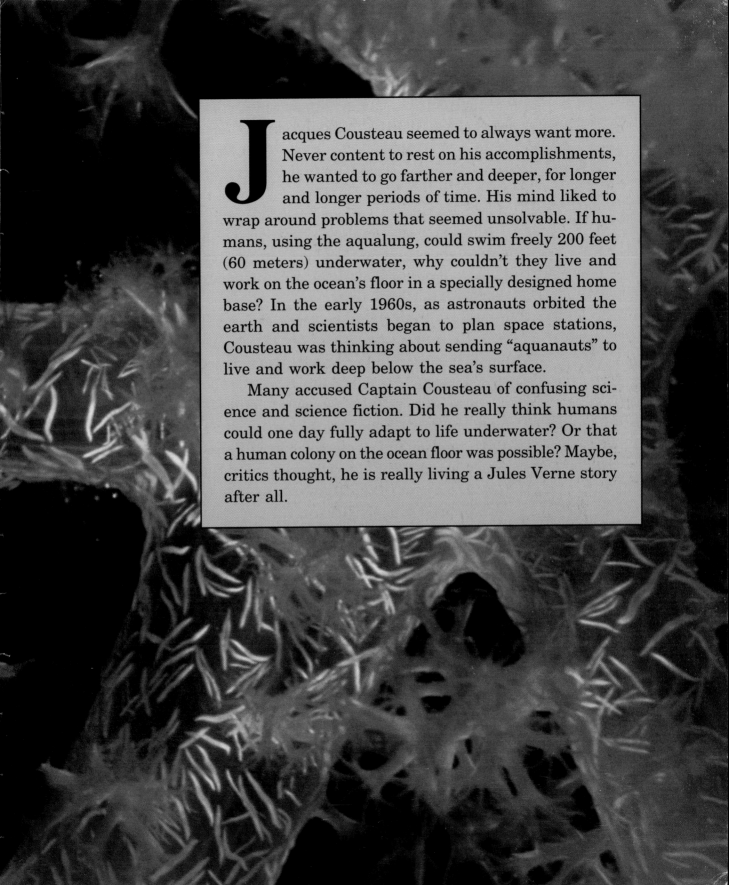

Jacques Cousteau seemed to always want more. Never content to rest on his accomplishments, he wanted to go farther and deeper, for longer and longer periods of time. His mind liked to wrap around problems that seemed unsolvable. If humans, using the aqualung, could swim freely 200 feet (60 meters) underwater, why couldn't they live and work on the ocean's floor in a specially designed home base? In the early 1960s, as astronauts orbited the earth and scientists began to plan space stations, Cousteau was thinking about sending "aquanauts" to live and work deep below the sea's surface.

Many accused Captain Cousteau of confusing science and science fiction. Did he really think humans could one day fully adapt to life underwater? Or that a human colony on the ocean floor was possible? Maybe, critics thought, he is really living a Jules Verne story after all.

In 1962, Cousteau, unfazed by criticism, devoted his energies to the Conshelf experiment. (The name "Conshelf" is short for Continental Shelf Station.) This project proposed to show that humans could not only survive at the sea's bottom, they could live and work there as well.

Conshelf was to be the beginning of a new era in human development, Jacques felt. He could, he wrote, foresee hundreds of thousands of aquanauts living and working half their lives under the sea. "More important than the huge space and wealth," he said, "they will draw new thoughts and creativity from a whole new world. And hopefully we may enter an era that deserves the title, civilization."[21]

In February 1962, astronaut John Glenn first orbited the earth. Seven months later, on September 14, 1962, two aquanauts named Albert Falco and Claude Wesly swam to a big yellow cylinder that had been towed to a spot in the Mediterranean near Marseilles and dropped to a shelf 35 feet (11 meters) underwater. They entered their new "home" and prepared to stay for one week.

Life wasn't dull for the first two aquanauts. Each day they left the station and dove deeper to perform more experiments. They monitored radio and TV hookups with the surface, and they were visited often by Captain Cousteau and many doctors and journalists. Everyone wanted to know how these two would fare. They were, after all, the first humans to experience a long period of weightlessness since vertebrates had moved from sea to land some 500 million years earlier.

When the two aquanauts came to the surface, they'd suffered few physical effects. However, the experience of solitude and weightlessness had clearly left a mark

Cousteau's submarine in the museum of the Oceanographic Institute of Monaco

Cousteau on the Conshelf project, monitoring the crew's activities through radio and TV hookups

on them. As Falco told Cousteau when he emerged, "I don't know exactly what has happened. I am the same person, yet I am no longer the same. Under the sea everything is— . . . everything is moral."[22]

The Conshelf experiment left an impression on Captain Cousteau, too. A new kind of man is coming into being, he told the World Congress on Underwater Activities a few months later. "Diving has gone beyond sport; it is now a worldwide movement. . . . We are now moving toward an alteration of human anatomy to give man almost unlimited freedom underwater."[23]

Conshelf II followed in 1963. This time there were five aquanauts, and their star-shaped vessel was plunged deeper into the sea—the Red Sea—and for a longer period of time. Experiments were conducted in the main vessel, called The *Starfish House*. Meanwhile, two aquanauts stayed in a rocket-shaped cabin breathing a mixture a helium and air. From the cabin, the two made deep-water dives for another experiment. They were testing to see whether a helium booster station might allow divers to make deeper dives without suffering the effects of rapture of the deep.

The rest of the scientific and medical crew, including Jacques and Simone Cousteau, were on board *Calypso*, anchored near the *Starfish House*. A production crew for a film about the experiment was also on

Cousteau explaining a drawing of his "spheric submarine base" for Conshelf III, in which five men would spend two weeks underwater

board *Calypso*, working and suffering in the extreme heat of the Middle East. The heat made work and even sleep very difficult. For everyone except the aquanauts themselves, Conshelf II was nothing short of a nightmare.

Still, the results of the experiment were impressive. The two deep-water aquanauts managed to dive to depths of 360 feet (110 meters). This proved Cousteau's notion that deeper free dives could be made from helium booster stations than from the water's surface. After a month, all seven men emerged in good shape. The film produced about Conshelf II, called *World Without Sun*, was also a success. In 1964 it won the Oscar award for best documentary film.

In planning Conshelf III, Captain Cousteau wanted to do away with the aquanauts' dependence on the surface base station, in this case *Calypso*. He worried that the lives and work of the aquanauts could be jeopardized by mistakes made on land or on board ship. Therefore the Conshelf III vessel was supplied with everything needed for a month's time. A compression and decompression area was designed for divers entering and leaving the vessel. Since normal compressed air couldn't be used at Conshelf III's depth, aquanauts breathed heliox, a mixture of helium and oxygen.

With a few glitches, Conshelf III proved to be a great success. There were a few stunning moments, such as when Conshelf's Philippe Cousteau—the captain's younger son—spoke via telephone with Scott Carpenter of *Sealab II*, the U.S. Navy's experiment station. Conshelf was 328 feet (100 meters) below the surface of the Mediterranean; *Sealab* was 208 feet (63 meters) under the Pacific off the coast of southern California.

Medals of the French Legion of Honor, into which Cousteau was initiated in 1964

Cousteau welcomes Andre Laban, chief aboard the submarine house, as he emerges from the decompression chamber at the end of Conshelf III.

As Cousteau wrote about the experiment: "We had proved our point that man can occupy and exploit the sea bottom—by developing new technologies of high-pressure breathing apparatus [and] by keeping to a minimum the life-support ties to the surface. Perhaps most significant of all, we had begun to breed a new . . . sense of confidence. Our young men began to think into, to feel, the undersea environment."[24]

The film made about Conshelf III was never shown in theaters but instead became a television special. It was shown in the United States as "The World of Jacques Cousteau." This was the first of several specials produced with Hollywood's David L. Wolper and the National Geographic Society. Its success meant that other Cousteau specials would surely follow.

In fact, by 1966, all three of the major television networks were interested in broadcasting specials on the Cousteau expeditions. Jacques and his son Philippe, who at twenty-six was beginning to look and act like his father's right-hand man, traveled to New York to negotiate a TV contract. After weeks of talking, Cousteau signed a $4.2 million contract with ABC-TV to produce twelve one-hour TV films. The series would be called "The Undersea World of Jacques Cousteau."

This huge television contract changed everything in Jacques Cousteau's life. Now, after twenty-five years of exploring, he had the financial security to plan an expedition to the world's oceans. Since "The Undersea World of Jacques Cousteau" would run for four years, with three shows a year, he could plan far in advance.

ABC-TV president Thomas Moore (left), Cousteau, and producer David L. Wolper announcing the expedition that would result in the 12-part series "The Undersea World of Jacques Cousteau"

Jacques's film company, Les Requins Associes, or Sharks Associated, was responsible for shooting the material. All the other post-production work would be done by David Wolper Productions of Los Angeles. Philippe Cousteau was to act as mediator between the Cousteau organization and David Wolper. He would live in Los Angeles but jet constantly between there and New York and Paris and *Calypso*'s various remote locations.

It was a heady time for Jacques and Simone Cousteau's younger son. Tall and handsome, Philippe had cut quite a figure on his trip to New York with his father. He had sat in on the television negotiations and had made it clear he wanted to work closely with his father's interests. The Cousteaus' older son, Jean-Michel, had become an architect and was on the fringe of the Cousteau empire. Philippe was poised to become as accomplished, and maybe even as famous, as his father.

Jacques and Philippe during the filming of "The Undersea World of Jacques Cousteau"

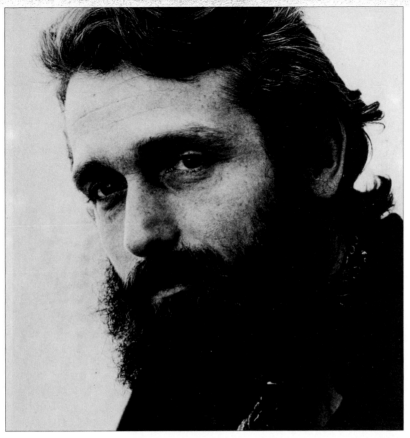

Philippe Cousteau

There was only one problem. In New York, during the time of the intense television negotiations between Jacques Cousteau and David Wolper and ABC-TV, Philippe had fallen in love with a lovely American fashion model. Her name was Janice Sullivan. She loved fashion and parties and had never even heard of Jacques Cousteau. Later in 1966, when the Cousteau family members were all back in France, Philippe announced that he and Janice wanted to get married. Jacques and Simone were ready with an answer: NO.

Jacques and Simone were outraged. They didn't want their son to get married—not yet. He had so much to contribute to his father's various undertakings, so much traveling to do. He was only twenty-six and so handsome and talented. And he couldn't marry an American fashion model who couldn't even speak French!

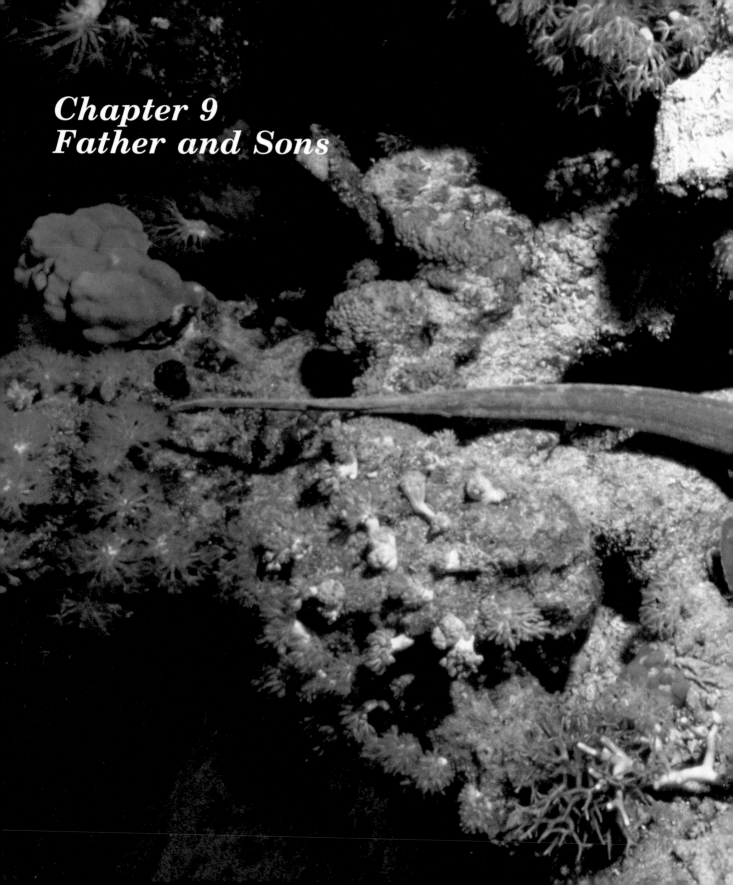

Chapter 9
Father and Sons

Philippe Cousteau didn't wait for his parents to change their minds about Janice. He listened to his mother tell him all the reasons he shouldn't marry her. Then he listened to his father, and in the end, he did exactly what he wanted. The couple were married in Paris in January 1967. Neither Jacques nor Simone attended the ceremony. They did send a wedding gift, though: a six-week crash course in French for their new American daughter-in-law.

Janice Cousteau said good-bye to her husband two weeks after their wedding. It was time, after all, to begin filming the new television series. Janice stayed in Paris, while Philippe joined his father at the production offices in Los Angeles.

The air was chilly between father and son. Philippe was angry and hurt at his parents' disapproval of his marriage. Jacques, though still upset at his son's stubbornness, wanted at least to resume a working relationship. For a while, though, silence was the rule.

February 1967 saw the launching of the newly refurbished *Calypso* from its home port in Monaco. No expense had been spared in readying the ship for the long journey ahead. The mission this time seemed almost a permanent one—or at least open-ended. With a long-term TV contract in hand, *Calypso*'s captain would explore the seas until he decided it was time to head home. Who knew when that would be? As *Calypso* sailed from Monaco, a huge crowd, including Princess Grace and Prince Rainier, waved and cheered.

Once *Calypso* reached the familiar waters of the Red Sea, the captain ordered the anchor dropped so the divers could test the new equipment. Nearly everything, in fact, was new: aqualungs, diving suits, electric scooters, underwater cameras, even the miles of electric cable had all been replaced.

Cousteau piloting the Calypso

As *Calypso* headed east, Philippe Cousteau was setting up his own location base in San Diego. There he would begin filming the migration of the California grey whales. Then he would follow the huge mammals to the quiet bays of Mexico's Baja Peninsula, where the females give birth and raise their young.

Filming for this all-important television series was an emotional roller coaster. The footage needed to be exciting—riveting—but, as usual with Captain Cousteau, safety had to come first. The shark sequences for the first installment were particularly stressful as cameramen tried to get as close as possible to the frightening creatures.

Calypso traveled from the Red Sea to the Indian Ocean, along Madagascar, the coast of Mozambique, and around South Africa's Cape of Good Hope. Philippe, halfway around the world, continued to film separate installments off the Baja Peninsula and in the Pacific. Jacques lived on board *Calypso*, although he went ashore frequently to catch a plane for France or America. In the winter of 1968, he flew to New York to promote the series debut, the stunning episode called simply "Sharks."

As millions began watching "The Undersea World of Jacques Cousteau" on television that winter, *Calypso* crossed the Atlantic to film first off Brazil's coast then in the Caribbean. As the series proceeded on schedule, the relationship between Jacques and Philippe deteriorated. Philippe resented his father for not giving him more responsibility. Jacques claimed Philippe needed to work harder if he wanted to one day take over the Cousteau organization. In 1969 Philippe had had enough. He moved permanently to Los Angeles with Jan and started his own film company.

Jacques and Jean-Michel Cousteau giving a press conference in 1971

In the meantime, Jacques and Simone's older son, Jean-Michel, began devoting more of his time to the television series. He seemed ready to take over Philippe's important role.

Jean-Michel and his wife, Anne-Marie, lived in Los Angeles, too, but they rarely saw Philippe and Jan. The two brothers and their wives had grown jealous of each other, especially over the question of who would one day be heir to their father's empire. Everyone had always assumed it would be Philippe. However, since his marriage to Jan and the falling-out with his parents, Jean-Michel seemed the more logical choice. Jacques would say nothing about the matter and seemed to enjoy the uncertainty.

Several years passed before, in the early 1970s, Jacques and Philippe could admit that they missed

Father and son

and needed each other. Jacques longed for Philippe's sound advice. Jean-Michel served well as a business and operations manager, but Philippe's verve and imagination were irreplaceable. The reconciliation was complete when, in 1976, Jan gave birth to the couple's first child, a daughter named Alexandra. The new grandparents were overjoyed.

Father and son then scouted out, separately, a place for themselves within the growing environmental movement. Jacques had become increasingly alarmed by the pollution of the world's oceans. Philippe, more a lover of wildlife than his father, decried the loss of many species' natural habitats. By the mid-1970s they both began using their considerable influence to affect government policy on environmental issues.

At this time Jacques founded the Cousteau Society. He became its president, and Philippe its vice-president. The society's three main goals were to influence politicians and world leaders, to support research, and to raise public awareness through the media, books, and education. Within a year, the Cousteau Society had 120,000 members and was engaged in several heated battles in the U.S. Congress. With the Cousteau Society, Jacques entered what he called a new phase in his life. Now, instead of battling the elements, he would battle the system.

In 1976, to everyone's surprise, ABC-TV decided to cancel the series. It had been successful, but according to executives, it no longer fit into the network's future plans. Jacques was disappointed but could take heart in the fact that the series was watched around the world.

Cousteau and one of his divers examining a small grouper, whose ancestor, Cousteau believes, may have swallowed the biblical Jonah

Jacques soon worked out an agreement with the Public Broadcasting Service for a new show called "Cousteau Odyssey." This series continued to focus on the exploration of the world's seas. Meanwhile, another—more controversial—show, "Oasis in Space," went into production. "Oasis" dealt with subjects such as pollution, population control, and world hunger.

As Jacques crisscrossed America and the world, giving speeches and lectures and attending rallies, he began to long for a research center in the United States, where the Cousteau Society could concentrate its various endeavors. By the end of 1978, several sites on the East Coast were being considered—Norfolk, Virginia, and St. Petersburg and Miami, Florida. Norfolk was eventually selected as the home of the society's research and educational center.

Meanwhile, Philippe had completed a year-long study of the condition of the Mediterranean Sea. Now he had begun a similar project on the Nile River in Egypt. He and a film crew spent months traveling up and down the long river, collecting facts about pollution levels and animal habitats.

Philippe was an expert pilot and sailor. For most of his research and filmmaking, he liked to use a PBY—a kind of flying ship—which had been christened the *Flying Calypso*.

In late June 1979, Philippe had just finished visiting the Nile and was bringing the *Flying Calypso* into Lisbon, Portugal. As usual when landing a PBY, he looked for a stretch of straight river. He found one on the Tagus River, near the Lisbon suburb of Aberca. He'd landed the *Flying Calypso* hundreds of times and felt that, if conditions were right, almost nothing could go wrong.

Portuguese navy divers carrying the covered body of Philippe Cousteau, which they recovered from the Tagus River

As he approached the Tagus, the *Flying Calypso*'s bottom touched the water with a reassuring thud. Then, as it's supposed to, it bounced back up, then landed more softly. On the second landing, though, the plane hit something, flipped over, and tore apart. In a few seconds all was quiet.

Local fishermen helped the stunned passengers from the wreckage. When one of the dazed crew members looked first at the sinking plane and then at the passengers huddled in fishing boats, he realized something was terribly wrong: Philippe was missing.

The Cousteau family arrived in Lisbon from all parts of the world and huddled together, grief-stricken, while local authorities dredged the river. Three days after the crash, Philippe's body was recovered. A brief

The casket of Philippe Cousteau, moments before his burial at sea off the Portuguese coast. Standing by is his widow, Janice.

funeral service was held in Lisbon. The flag-draped coffin was taken several miles out into the Atlantic for a burial at sea. Philippe's widow and daughter then left Lisbon for California. There, a few months later, Janice Cousteau gave birth to a son, whom she named Philippe Pierre Jacques-Yves Cousteau.

Jacques Cousteau put on a brave face for the press, giving thanks that the copilot escaped with only minor injuries. "That is fate," Jacques said many times. "We must accept it and go on." He stressed that the schedule for the newest television series would not be affected, that all would go on as before. But no one—including the captain himself—believed that. For both Jacques and the Cousteau organization, everything had changed.

Chapter 10
The Next Generation

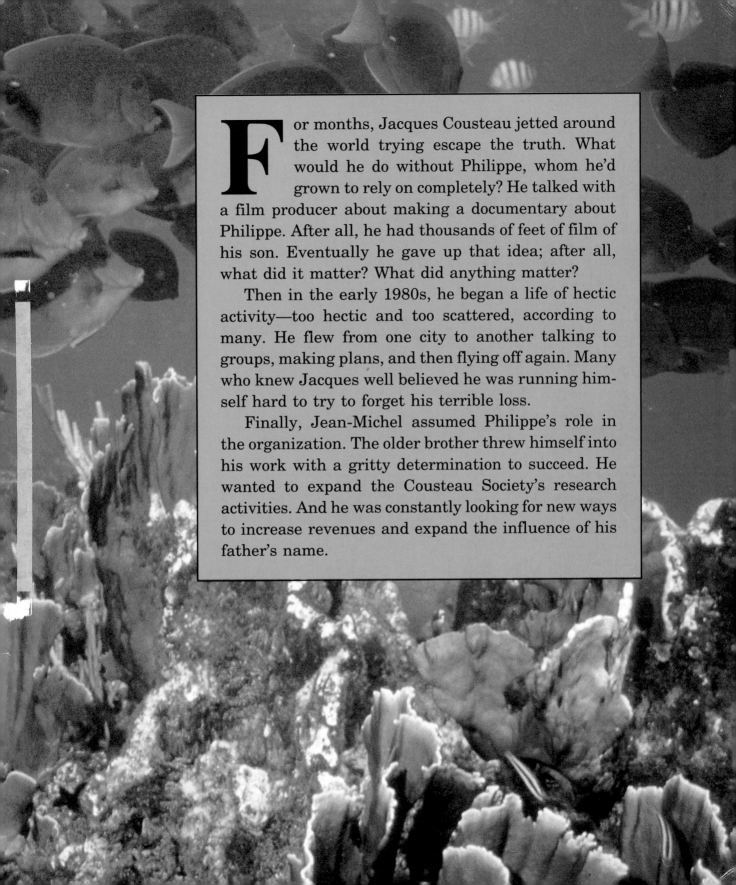

For months, Jacques Cousteau jetted around the world trying escape the truth. What would he do without Philippe, whom he'd grown to rely on completely? He talked with a film producer about making a documentary about Philippe. After all, he had thousands of feet of film of his son. Eventually he gave up that idea; after all, what did it matter? What did anything matter?

Then in the early 1980s, he began a life of hectic activity—too hectic and too scattered, according to many. He flew from one city to another talking to groups, making plans, and then flying off again. Many who knew Jacques well believed he was running himself hard to try to forget his terrible loss.

Finally, Jean-Michel assumed Philippe's role in the organization. The older brother threw himself into his work with a gritty determination to succeed. He wanted to expand the Cousteau Society's research activities. And he was constantly looking for new ways to increase revenues and expand the influence of his father's name.

Jacques and Jean-Michel playing with a rare giant river otter during their Amazon expedition

Throughout the 1980s, the projects and expeditions continued. One was a very ambitious journey deep into the heart of the Amazon rain forest, sponsored by Ted Turner's cable television network. Another was an expedition up the Mississippi River. In 1985, Cousteau launched a five-year voyage around the world. This resulted in a television series called "Rediscovery of the World."

To this day, Jacques remains ever the activist, working hard, pouring all his energy into saving the lovely blue planet called Earth. In the 1990s, he has continued producing environmental films. And a top priority has been his goal of gathering twenty million signatures worldwide for his "bill of rights for future generations."

Cousteau beaming from the deck of the newly-refurbished Calypso *before beginning his Rediscovery voyage*

Now in his eighties, Captain Cousteau reflects on the state of the world, on the seas, on other explorers. He tries hard, however, never to reflect on himself. Self-analysis doesn't lead one to explore new places; it holds one back, he believes. He keeps moving and working and trying to make people think. In 1985, when he began his Rediscovery voyage, an interviewer asked him what this ambitious journey might mean for the Cousteau legacy:

Is this a summing up? the interviewer asked.

"No, nothing is finished for me."

A turning point?

"No, I keep going straight."

A stage in life?

"I don't stop. . . ."[25]

Appendix

Aquanauts inside Cousteau's diving saucer

Cousteau, director of the Oceanographic Museum of Monaco, with Princess Grace and Prince Rainier at the opening of a 1962 exhibition "Man beneath the Sea"

Cousteau is received into the prestigious French Academy—
Paris, 1989. Behind him is Academy member
Leopold Sedar Senghor, former president of Senegal.

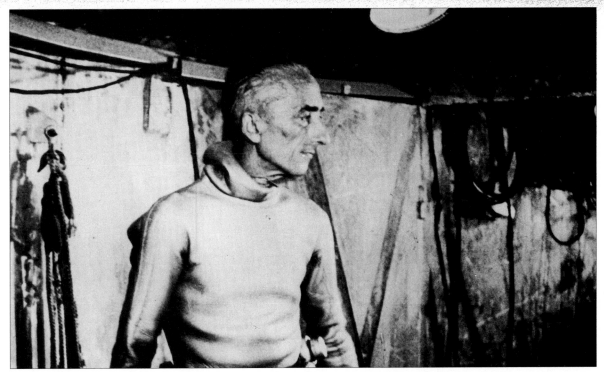

Cousteau in a still shot from his 1965 film "World Without Sun"

A student requests Cousteau's autograph during a
1970 ceremony at the University of California at Berkeley.

Cousteau meets with U.S. Secretary of State James Baker
during a trip to Washington in 1989.

Cousteau meets with French president François Mitterrand in Paris in May 1991.

Timeline of Events in Cousteau's Lifetime

1910—Jacques-Yves Cousteau is born in St. André-de-Cubzac, France, on June 11

1929—Cousteau graduates from high school with honors

1930—Cousteau enters the French Naval Academy at Brest

1932-33—Cousteau sails around the world on the navy training ship *Jeanne D'Arc*

1933—Cousteau enters the French Navy's aviation school

1936—Cousteau is badly injured in a car accident; he makes his first undersea dive; in Paris, he meets and falls in love with Simone Melchior

1937—Jacques and Simone are married

1938—The Cousteaus' first child, Jean-Michel, is born

1939—World War II begins; France and Great Britain declare war on Germany; Jacques begins service aboard the *Dupleix*

1940—Hitler's forces invade France and bomb Paris; the Cousteaus' second child, Philippe, is born

1942—Hitler invades the Toulon naval base

1943—Cousteau first experiences "rapture of the deep"; he and Emile Gagnan develop and test the aqualung; he produces his first film, *Par dix-huit mètres du fond (18 Meters Down)*

1944—Cousteau shows the aqualung to the Allied Navy; Allies invade France's Normandy coast; France is liberated from German control

1945—World War II ends

1946—Cousteau conducts deep-diving experiments in the Fountain of Vaucluse near Avignon, France

1947—Cousteau and fellow divers risk the dangers of rapture of the deep and set new depth records, but diver Maurice Fargues dies in his attempt

1948—With Auguste Piccard, Cousteau tests the bathyscaphe

1950—Cousteau becomes president of the French Oceanographic Campaigns and commander of the research vessel *Calypso*

1951—Cousteau takes the *Calypso* to the Red Sea on its first expedition

1952—Cousteau travels to New York to gain support for *Calypso* missions; the *Calypso* salvages treasure from a sunken ancient Roman freighter; the National Geographic Society and other organizations agree to fund Cousteau expeditions; Jean-Pierre Serventi dies on a dive

1953—Cousteau publishes his book *The Silent World*

1954—On the *Calypso*'s second mission, Cousteau and crew explore for oil sources in the Gulf of Oman

1955—*Calypso* goes to Assumption Island in the Indian Ocean for its third expedition

1956—*Le Monde du Silence* (*The Silent World*), co-directed by Cousteau and Louis Malle, wins the top award at the Cannes Film Festival

1957—*The Silent World* wins an Academy Award for best documentary; Cousteau becomes director of the Oceanographic Museum of Monaco and head of the Conshelf Saturation Dive Program; he resigns from the French navy

1959—Cousteau travels to New York on the *Calypso* to attend the first World Oceanographic Congress

1960—With Monaco's Prince Rainier, Cousteau opposes France's dumping of radioactive wastes into the Mediterranean; Cousteau speaks against nuclear waste disposal before the World Underwater Federation

1961—President John F. Kennedy presents Cousteau with the National Geographic Society's gold medal

1962—Cousteau conducts his first Conshelf experiment, in which two aquanauts spend a week underwater

1963—In Conshelf II experiments, aquanauts find that a helium booster station enables them to make deeper dives

1964—*World Without Sun*, Cousteau's film about Conshelf II, wins an Academy Award for best documentary

1965—Conshelf III divers spend a month underwater

1966—Cousteau and ABC-TV sign a contract to produce a twelve-episode TV series, "The Undersea World of Jacques Cousteau"

1967—Over his parents' objections, Philippe Cousteau marries American model Janice Sullivan; *Calypso* leaves Monaco for the Red Sea

1969—Their relations strained, Philippe parts with Jacques and starts his own film company in Los Angeles

1976—Jacques and Philippe begin working together again, concentrating on environmental issues; a daughter, Alexandra, is born to Philippe and Jan

1979—Philippe Cousteau is killed when his vessel the *Flying Calypso* flips over in the Tagus River near Lisbon, Portugal; his widow gives birth to a son, Philippe Pierre Jacques-Yves Cousteau

1982—Sponsored by Ted Turner's cable television network, Cousteau makes an expedition to explore the Amazon River region

1983—Cousteau and the *Calypso* explore the Mississippi River

1985—In the refurbished *Calypso*, Cousteau begins a five-year, around-the-world voyage, called Rediscovery of the World, to study the relationship between people and the world's oceans

1989—Cousteau is admitted into the distinguished French Academy

1991—Cousteau launches a campaign to obtain 20 million signatures on his proposed "bill of rights for future generations"

1992—Cousteau presents a new environmental film at the worldwide Earth Summit in Rio de Janeiro, Brazil, and appeals to world leaders to protect the environment

Glossary of Terms

aqualung—A breathing device that enables a diver to stay underwater for long periods of time

aquanaut—A scuba diver who lives for a long period of time underwater

archipelago—A group or chain of islands

bathyscaphe—A vessel for deep-sea exploration that has a watertight sphere on its bottom

bends—Also called decompression sickness; pain, breathing problems, and paralysis due to nitrogen bubbles forming in the blood when an underwater diver rises to the surface too fast

bosun—(short for "boatswain") A ship's officer responsible for maintaining and repairing the ship's hull

christen—To baptize, name, or dedicate

cinematographer—A movie cameraman

decompression—A decrease in pressure, such as when a diver rises to the surface

documentary—A film presenting objective, factual information

grouper—A large fish that lives near the bottom of warm, saltwater seas

hangar—A shelter where aircraft or ships are repaired

idyllic—Pleasant, peaceful, and simple

melodrama—An overly dramatic and emotional play or movie

minesweeper—A ship that removes underwater explosives

prototype—A newly designed device to serve as an example for later models

radioactive fallout—Harmful particles that drift down through the atmosphere after a nuclear test

rapture of the deep—Another name for nitrogen narcosis; a feeling of high spirits and loss of a sense of reality caused by too much nitrogen entering the bloodstream during deep dives

scuba diving—("scuba" stands for self-contained underwater breathing apparatus) Deep diving using air tanks and a hose for breathing

tarpaulin—A large, often waterproof cloth for covering or shielding objects

Notes

[1] From *The Silent World* by Jacques-Yves Cousteau with Frederic Dumas, pp. 111-112. Copyright © 1953 by Harper & Brothers; copyright © renewed 1981 by Jacques-Yves Cousteau. Excerpts reprinted by permission of HarperCollins Publishers Inc.

[2] From *Cousteau: An Unauthorized Biography* by Axel Madsen, p. 8. Copyright © 1986 by Axel Madsen. Excerpts reprinted by permission of Beaufort Books Publishers.

[3] Ibid., p. 8.

[4] *The Silent World*, p. 9.

[5] Ibid., p. 34.

[6] *Cousteau: An Unauthorized Biography*, p. 44.

[7] *The Silent World*, p. 69.

[8] Ibid., p. 73.

[9] Ibid., p. 76.

[10] Ibid., p. 191.

[11] Ibid., p. 192.

[12] Ibid., pp. 192-193.

[13] Ibid., pp. 256-257.

[14] From *The Living Sea* by Jacques-Yves Cousteau with James Dugan, p. 22. Copyright © 1963 by Harper & Row, Publishers, Inc.; copyright © renewed 1991 by Jacques-Yves Cousteau and James Dugan. Excerpts reprinted by permision of HarperCollins Publishers Inc.

[15] Ibid., p. 23.

[16] *Cousteau: An Unauthorized Biography*, p. 70.

[17] Ibid., p. 70.

[18] Ibid., p. 92.

[19] *The Living Sea*, p. 153.

[20] Ibid.

[21] *Cousteau: An Unauthorized Biography*, p. 127.

[22] *The Living Sea*, p. 325.

[23] *Cousteau: An Unauthorized Biography*, p. 128.

[24] From *The Ocean World of Jacques Cousteau: Oasis in Space* by Jacques-Yves Cousteau, p. 127. Copyright © 1972 by Jacques-Yves Cousteau. New York: The World Publishing Company, Times Mirror.

[25] *Cousteau: An Unauthorized Biography*, p. 238.

Bibliography

For further reading, see:

Cousteau, Jacques-Yves. *The Living Sea*. NY: Harper & Row, 1963.

——. *The Ocean World of Jacques Cousteau*. Vol. 1, *Oasis in Space*. Suffern, NY: The Danbury Press, 1972.

——, with Frederic Dumas. *The Silent World*. NY: Harper & Brothers, 1953.

Greene, Carol. *Jacques Cousteau: Man of the Oceans*. Chicago: Childrens Press, 1990. (For younger readers)

Madsen, Axel. *Cousteau: An Unauthorized Biography*. NY: Beaufort Books, 1986.

Munson, Richard. *Cousteau: The Captain and His World*. NY: William Morrow, 1989.

Verne, Jules. *Twenty Thousand Leagues Under the Sea*. (There are many editions from many different publishers.)

Index

Page numbers in boldface type indicate illustrations.

Picture Identifications for Chapter Opening Spreads

6-7—Raccoon butterflyfish
16-17—Vineyards in the Bordeaux region of France
24-25—A brittle star on a sponge
36-37—Elkhorn coral
46-47—A school of bigeyes
62-63—French grunts in the Caribbean
76-77—Strange fish
90-91—Soft coral in the Red Sea
100-101—Blue-spotted stingray in the Red Sea
110-111—Fish in the Caribbean

Picture Acknowledgments

© **Agence France Presse**: 118 (top); Clement—118 (bottom)
AP/Wide World Photos—23, 31, 33, 34, 35, 41, 44, 55, 70, 72, 74, 85, 86, 93, 96, 97, 99, 104, 105, 106, 108, 109, 112, 113, 115, 116, 117 (top)
© **Cameramann International, Ltd.**—65
Dembinsky Photo Associates: © Marilyn Kazmers—14; © SharkSong/ M. Kazmers, 67, 83, 90-91
Steven Gaston Dobson—Cover illustration
Courtesy of The French Cultural Services, New York—95
© Bob Marinace—19
Photo by J. Baylor Roberts, © National Geographic Society—89
Official U.S. Navy Photograph—45
North Wind Picture Archives—29, 78
Odyssey Productions: © Robert Frerck—11, 15, 27, 43, 60, 61, 110-111; © Walter Frerck—2
PhotoEdit: © Alan Oddie—16-17
© **Porterfield/Chickering**—87, 92
R/C Photo Agency: © Richard L. Capps—21
H. Armstrong Roberts—30
Root Resources: 75; © Norbert Wu—24-25
Royal Geographical Society, London: 4
Tom Stack & Associates: 5; © Ron Church—114; © Garoutte/Bay Islands—12; © Brian Parker—36-37, 50, 58, 62-63, 73; © Ed Robinson—13; © Mike Severns—76-77; © Denise Tackett—46-47
UPI/Bettmann—39, 54, 56, 57, 64, 71, 94, 98, 102, 117 (bottom)
Valan Photos: © R. Berchin—6-7; © Fred Bravendam—81, 100-101; © Paul L. Janosi—8, 49, 59, 68, 69; © Robert Lasalle—10; © Richard Nowitz—18, 40; © Joyce Photographics—28

About the Author

Susan Sinnott began her publishing career as an editor for *Cricket*, a children's magazine. She later worked at the University of Wisconsin Press, where she managed and edited academic journals. Eventually, her own two children helped her to rediscover the joys of reading, writing, and editing books for young readers. For Childrens Press, Ms. Sinnott has written *Zebulon Pike* and *Extraordinary Hispanic Americans*. She lives in rattly old house in Portsmouth, New Hampshire, where she can sit at her desk and look out at the lovely harbor .